The Little Gray Home i

D1427532

A young Irish trade union organiser returns home from Manchester for his father's funeral in the west of Ireland, only to find himself involved in a train of events that leads him over the Northern Irish border to his terrifying death at the hands of the 'security forces'. Culminating in the savage confusion of 1971, the year of internment, *The Little Gray Home in the West* is a fast-moving satirical melodrama, black and hilarious by turns, drawing out the tangled web of the still-continuing Irish conflict. It is a revised version of D'Arcy and Arden's *Ballygombeen Bequest*, which had to be withdrawn in the face of a libel action.

Margaretta D'Arcy is Irish and has worked with improvisational and theatre techniques since the fifties. She is the Irish correspondent for the Polish theatre journal Dialog. *Her work with Arden includes* The Business of Good Government (*1960*), The Happy Haven (*1960*), Ars Longa, Vita Brevis (*1963*), Friday's Hiding (*1965*), The Royal Pardon (*1966*), Muggins is a Martyr (*1968*), The Hero Rises Up (*1968*), The Ballygombeen Bequest (*1972*), The Island of the Mighty (*1972*), Keep the People Moving (*for radio, 1972*), The Non-Stop Connolly Show (*1975*), Vandaleur's Folly (*1978*) *and* The Little Gray Home in the West (*1978*). *Her play* A Pinprick of History *was performed at the Almost Free Theatre, London in 1977.*

John Arden was born in Barnsley, Yorkshire, in 1930. While studying architecture at Cambridge and Edinburgh universities, he began to write plays, four of which have been produced at the Royal Court Theatre: The Waters of Babylon, Live Like Pigs, Serjeant Musgrave's Dance *and* The Happy Haven; *while a fifth,* The Workhouse Donkey, *was produced at the Festival Theatre, Chichester. For a year he held an Annual Fellowship in Playwriting at Bristol University, and Bristol Old Vic produced* Ironhand, *his free adaptation of Goethe's* Goetz von Berlichingen. Armstrong's Last Goodnight *was first produced at the Glasgow Citizens' Theatre and later at the National Theatre.* Left-Handed Liberty *was specially commissioned by the Corporation of London to commemorate the 750th Anniversary of Magna Carta and was produced at the Mermaid Theatre. He is married to Margaretta D'Arcy with whom he has collaborated on several plays. Arden's first novel,* Silence Among the Weapons (*1982*), *was short-listed for the Booker-McConnell Prize for Fiction.*

Margaretta D'Arcy and **John Arden**

The Little Gray Home in the West

An Anglo-Irish Melodrama

A Methuen Paperback

A Methuen Modern Play

First published in 1982 by Pluto Press Ltd,
Published in 1986, in Great Britain by Methuen London Ltd,
11 New Fetter Lane, London EC4P 4EE
and in the United States of America
by Methuen Inc. 29 West 35th Street, New York, NY 10001
Copyright © 1982, 1986 by Margaretta D'Arcy and John Arden

British Cataloguing in Publication Data

D'Arcy, Margaretta
  The little gray home in the west: an
  Anglo-Irish melodrama.
  I. Title   II. Arden, John
  822'.914   PR6054.A695

  ISBN 0–413–40300–9

Typeset by Grassroots Typeset, London NW6
Printed in Great Britain by
Fletcher & Son Ltd, Norwich

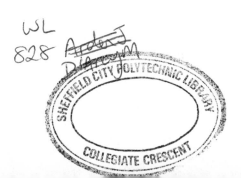

A note on intended performances

In the spring of 1978 we paid a visit to Greece, where we met many theatre people. During one of our conversations we spoke about the role of women in Greek classical theatre, as seen by modern Greek actresses in the aftermath of the Fascist Colonels' junta. Women, we were told, practically never had a chance to play roles of 'power', 'social authority', 'decision-making', because of the structure of the ancient plays and their importance in the 20th century repertory. Much the same, we realised, could be said of Shakespeare in Britain. So long as men were always cast as gods, tyrants, heroes, the sexual attitudes that had lain behind the military coup in Greece could only be reinforced by cultural conventions. If Aeschylus, Sophocles and Euripides had written women's parts for men to play because of the social conditions of their age, why by the same token could not their men's parts in our age be played by women? So many of the Greek actresses are artists of great strength and intensity: and we could so easily see them in such roles as Oedipus or Orestes. Once again the Shakespearian analogy came to mind.

The following year D'Arcy attended a workshop at an all day 'Women-in-Entertainment' seminar in London. Here she spoke about what the Greek actresses had told her and put forward the suggestion that male domination of the professional theatre was largely due to the uncritical acceptance of sexual type-casting — that men did not have to play men, as a rule of nature, just as it is not necessary to find a hunchback for Richard III or a dotard for King Lear; that the response of male actors to roles of cruelty, rapacity, violence and military force was extremely equivocal and tended to fortify an unseemly romanticism towards such undesirable social tendencies; and that the 'sexual authority' of even benevolent male roles was unduly strengthened by inevitable male casting. In a society where women's lives are still largely subservient to men's, it is not realistic to expect dramatists to write only idealised portraits of dominant women in order to redress the balance: plays must deal with life *as it is* quite as much as life *as it should be*. But if audiences were to receive the playwrights' pictures of sexual dominance interpreted not by the dominators but by the dominated, could not a new kind of criticism of received attitudes result from what might superficially seem to be merely a new directors' gimmick? This notion went down very well with Women-in-Entertainment: it was instinctively seen to be a vital ingredient in any revision of patriarchal culture in the theatre, and it is to be hoped that the well argued paper may yet be written on the subject. Be that as it may, as we are playwrights and in control of the destinies of our work (thanks to the hard-fought battles of the Threatre Writers' Union) we intend that *The Little Gray Home in the West* shall be a contribution to the attempt to get rid of the *machismo* glamourizing of imperialism and militarism on our boards.

When this play is performed by a professional company, the male parts are to be played by women.

Margaretta D'Arcy and John Arden
Galway, Ireland
August 1981

Notes on the authors

Margaretta D'Arcy comes from Dublin, where she obtained her early experience in the theatre. She has worked in the theatre consistently since 1951 and is co-author of many scripts for stage, radio and TV. Her most recent published work includes: *Tell Them Everything* (Pluto Press) — an account of the three months she spent in Armagh Women's Jail in 1980; *Vandaleur's Folly* (Eyre Methuen); and *The Non-Stop Connolly Show* (Pluto Press) — plays about Anglo-Irish history and social conflict, written in collaboration with John Arden. She lives in Galway and has been working on a series of TV/film dramas, chiefly dealing with various aspects of contemporary Irish life. Her stage play *A Pinprick of History* — a surreal examination of the Irish general election of 1977 — was produced at the Almost Free theatre that same year. She is the Irish correspondent of the international theatre review published by *Dialog* magazine (Warsaw).

John Arden was born in Barnsley, Yorkshire. He began full-time theatre writing in 1958 for the Royal Court, London. He is the author of *Serjeant Musgrave's Dance, Armstrong's Last Goodnight* etc. A collection of his essays on the theatre, *To Present the Pretence*, was published in 1978 by Eyre Methuen. Recent works include several radio plays: *Pearl* (published by Eyre Methuen); *Don Quixote* (a two-part adaptation of Cervantes's novel); *Garland for a Hoar Head* (shortly to be performed by BBC). He has completed a novel, *Silence Among the Weapons*, to be published by Eyre Methuen.

Acknowledgements

We would like to express our gratitude to Gerry O'Neill, who made his theatre (The Sugawn, off Balls Pond Road, Highbury, North London) available for the first reading of *The Little Gray Home in the West* on 1 May 1978.

And also to the following people, who took part in the reading:
John Blanchard
Terry Dougherty
Don Foley
John Joyce
Michael Loughnan
Anne O'Connor
Timothy O'Grady
Treasa Ní Fhátharta
John Quinn
Stephen Rea
Roger Sloman

(John Joyce, Stephen Rea and Roger Sloman were in the original 7:84 production of *The Ballygombeen Bequest* which was taken off because of a libel action in 1972.)

They all gave their services free and the greatest appreciation is due to them for their act of solidarity and trust in the play.

Margaretta D'Arcy
John Arden

List of characters

Baker-Fortescue	a business man
Crotchet	a solicitor
Seamus O'Leary	a smallholder
Teresa	his wife
Padraic	his son
Siobhan	his daughter
Hagan	a contractor
Limegrave	an agent of British Military Intelligence
Butler McReek	an agent of Irish Political Police
Mulholland	of the Republican Movement in the West of Ireland
An Intelligence Officer	
A Corporal	of the British Army
A Private	

The action of the play takes place in Britain and Ireland between nineteen forty-five and nineteen seventy-one.

Airs to songs: The titles of the traditional ballad-airs are given only as a rough guide. Other tunes of the same type may be found more suitable for particular performers or particular circumstances of production. Also it may be necessary to adapt the airs slightly here and there to give the words of the songs the fullest emphasis. This should always be done in preference to adapting the words to the music.

ACT ONE
Scene One

Enter PADRAIC *as a dead man.*

Padraic

Between England and Ireland to this day is so great quarrel,
To introduce it in a play I know well is to keel the barrel
Of old dried blood and new wet blood
And steaming pitch and shit and rancorous deep complaint
And altogether such a poisonous flood
As sure would make a cannibal cyclops faint
For very stink of it: and yet I have no choice.
This is my only voice.
For I am dead and murdered. Out of my grave
I cannot walk alive
Except in an actor's mask. My tongue in another's throat
Explaining, arguing, persuading fruitlessly how it should all come
    about
That I am dead and cannot walk alive upon my own
And yet for nothing that I myself had done
For only that which I myself had been
In life before my life, before I was even born...

Padraic O'Leary: died under stress of inhuman and degrading
treatment — but in no sense *torture* — nineteen seventy-one. At the
age of twenty-six. Having returned home to the west of Ireland
after ten years in the north of England, where I worked on the
buildings and learned about class-struggle, where I joined a trade
union and learned about solidarity, where I adhered to a socialist
party and learned that colonialism in my own country, resistance to
it, armed struggle, the republican movement, were symptoms of
nineteenth century political atavism and that no-one opened their
mouths about 'em but a crowd of backward paddies... I was then
to discover that my journey home again from Liverpool had been
anticipated the year of my birth by another man's doomed travel-
ling. He went for the same reason — as the result of a death, for a
testament, a bequest. Here he is.

THE LAST LEGATEE OF THE OLD DISPENSATION
RECEIVES HIS INHERITANCE: NINETEEN FORTY-FIVE.

Enter BAKER-FORTESCUE, *wearing dark glasses.*

Baker-Fortescue Good day to you. Baker-Fortescue at your service. Roderick Baker-Fortescue — the Honourable Roderick Baker-Fortescue, for what such a handle is worth — financially not too much — but... Ha h'm: released, very recently released — five minutes ago, in fact, from patriotic wartime service, in a department of government which must alas remain nameless — security, the nod-and-the wink...

He takes off his dark glasses and replaces them with a business-executive's horn-rims.

Observe my glasses, no longer dark but clear and bright.
The war is over. Democracy has won the long long fight.
Padraic
Nineteen hundred and forty-five:
Not only the backroom boys are glad to be alive.
Baker-Fortescue Mind you, a most productive and advantageous back room for some of us. Oh, not exactly military intelligence... not military at all, as a matter of fact... departmentally very very closely connected. Germany, Italy, rehabilitation of responsible government under the guidance of the allied occupying powers — you will readily understand commodities of all sorts in very very short supply. Currency, coupons, immeasurable bumph: moreover some most remunerative sidelines in relation to the investigation of war-crimes, the political past of public figures, wrap it up, keep it smooth, united front against the *Reds*, and above all re-establish regular commercial communications. Co-ordinating thus our national defence with my personal advantage, I have returned home highly confident that my own business in Harrogate — export-import cost-price intimate novelties — will not have suffered in my absence: my partner tells me my new European contacts will add enormously to future activities. None the less I must break myself in slowly to the diminuendo of British life as infected by socialism, though Comrade Attlee's new government is not yet, perhaps, *red*: sub-fusc would be a better word. I'll go to my club and look out for some refreshment.

PADRAIC *as a club-servant, hands him a bundle of letters.*

Aha, as I thought, no end of letters awaiting me. The world of legitimate business resumes its cohesive flow... From a solicitor — ho ho...?

I am not rich, but I have always found
That where a lawyer creeps upon the ground
Profits accrue, emoluments abound.
Whatever news he sends me by this post
I have no fear but I shall soon acquire
Some crafty carving-knife with which to rule the roast!

I am, you see, a business-man:
I look to the main chance where I can.

Reading the letter:

Good God: I have inherited property! My distant relative the Marquess of Ballydehob deceased. Bricks and mortar, fertile acreage, productive land — a sight more appropriate to the name of Baker-Fortescue than a scruffy little office in Harrogate: ha, a stake in the country! *Which* country? Ireland. God help us... A castle in the boglands of Munster. Rotten purlins in the roof, nettles and thistles in the cracks of the stonework, hired assassins I suppose, taking cover in the park? No, no, a dead loss, I'll not accept, I'll sell. Wait a moment, not even a castle... My spectacles, typing error...? Goddammit, the word is *chalet*. The Chalet, Kil — Kilna — something — Kilnasleeveen indeed. And fifteen acres. You can't call fifteen acres a park. A paddock perhaps. And what's this about a small-holding? 'The small-holding locally known as the Tintawndub, at present believed occupied by Seamus O'Leary Esq...' You know I very much doubt whether a character called Seamus could possibly have any right to style himself Esquire. Be that as it may, it appears he is to be my tenant. Oh-oh though, what's this? 'The validity of Mr O'Leary's title to the Tintawndub is open to variant interpretation...' 'Counsel's opinion...' No no no: indeed by God, no: I have inherited or not! I must see this attorney at once. What does he call himself? Croup, Croup, Crotchet, and Croup. The man I am to deal with will be Crotchet, I hope. At least, if he is, I shall not be outnumbered, ha!

Enter CROTCHET.

Mr Crotchet? Good morning. Baker-Fortescue.
Crotchet Delighted to make your acquaintance, Mr Fortescue.
Baker-Fortescue Baker-Fortescue.
Crotchet Please do sit down. Cold wind.
Baker-Fortescue Very cold.
Crotchet Blows from the left, I suppose. Not at all what we fought and died for. Coal, railways, steel, the Bank of England. Nationalise the lot. Even women, so they tell me.
Baker-Fortescue Good God, you don't say so.
Crotchet Oh yes, it's coming. *Levelling-down* is the accepted phrase, I believe. Hand over your lady-wife to —
Baker-Fortescue I am a bachelor.
Crotchet You'll do well to remain one. Because otherwise, hand her over to some sweaty-socked trade unionist and in return you'll be permitted on the first Friday of every month to avail yourself of the shared services of his slag-heap of a daughter... Import-export, I believe? Unless you're on permanent sub-contract to the State Authority for Public Misery, you'll have the lot commandeered by

the Chancellor of the Exchequer — the Commissar for Loot, I suppose they call him now. So this little legacy in Ireland will come in very useful. It's their Ireland, you know, not ours — I mean the neutral bit — *Eera*...? You a Catholic?

Baker-Fortescue Good God no.

Crotchet Much better not to be — over there you couldn't even offer your lady-wife a kiss without a certificate from the priest. If you had a lady-wife. And if you're going to live there. Are you going to live there?

Baker-Fortescue I hadn't really thought about it.

Crotchet You might have to in the end. I mean, there's no possibility of a Labour Government over there. The Bishops sit on *that* pot: oh, very firm posteriors the Bishops have, over there. But if *you* don't want to live there, there'll be very many who do. Delightful part of the country, they tell me. Fishing, rough shooting, horses, all that — no rationing over there. You should let the place to visitors — far from the madding crowd, the slow Boeotian charm of the vanishing peasantry — oh they touch their caps over there, pull the forelock, incredible, they still do it... never see anything like it in England again. People of your own class will pay twenty pound a week, for nothing at all really, except a bit of the old respect. I do recommend you to take the hint from my typing error, Castle instead of Chalet...

Baker-Fortescue That would hardly be the proper thing...?

Crotchet No no, the third Marquess did indeed have a fortified wall of some sort on the site... but it isn't architecture after all that your visitors will be looking for.

Baker-Fortescue What about this 'Tintawndub'?

Crotchet You mean the O'Learys? They seem to be a fixture. Perennial problem with inheritance through these Irish peerages. The Ballydehobs could never get rid of them. They add to the charm of the place. 'Faith and your honour's welcome to a day on the lake with the boat and 'tis meself will be after pointing out to you the locality of the big fish and the contrivances for catching them...'

Baker-Fortescue Begorrah...

Crotchet Oh yes... they don't pay rent.

Baker-Fortescue Then what *do* they pay? I mean they *are* on the property?

Crotchet Lord Ballydehob used to describe it as matter of good will. You want an old retainer — at least I'm sure your visitors could use one — so there you are — gratis. Pay them the odd half-crown, you see, in the way of baksheesh — not too much, mind, you could spoil them — make certain their cows don't wander into the Chalet — ask Mrs O'Leary to keep the place clean for you — and remind your visitors now and again to give them the odd half-crown. They'll do more good for your business than an illustrated article in the pages of *The Tatler*. But don't mention any question of rent.

It's rather a sore point in Kilnasleeveen.

Baker-Fortescue I don't understand.

Crotchet Lord Ballydehob's grandfather, on a visit to collect his rents, had his throat cut by the tenants — eighteen eighty-one.

Baker-Fortescue Good God.

Crotchet It's a long time ago. But you see, they don't forget.

Baker-Fortescue If that is the case, Mr Crotchet, it hardly seems to me a very secure investment. I mean, I am English, and a landowner, and a Protestant — I mean —

Crotchet

I don't think you'll find

That anyone will mind.

They need today the high-class tourist trade,

You bring them that and you are made.

With a shotgun and a fishing-rod

You will be worshipped like a god.

So long as you do not insist upon your legal right

You may live there in peace and never have to fight.

Consider yourself as a guest of the country.

They will treat you as though you were one of the gentry.

Baker-Fortescue I *am* one of the gentry.

Crotchet

It does not do to say so.

But be yourself and they will know.

Baker-Fortescue

Were they not neutral in our great war against dictatorship?

Crotchet

Not the kind of remark I advise you to let slip.

Baker-Fortescue

Is not the hand of De Valera stained red with British blood?

Crotchet

It has done him little good.

Not blood but British gold is what he needs today.

He will put that red hand in your hand

If you can but show him the way

To make rich his ramshackle kingdom

While you yourself are made rich.

Do you know O'Leary's great-grandfather

Had to lie down and die in a ditch?

Baker-Fortescue Good God, did he really?

Crotchet Oh yes, upon what is now *your* property — he always maintained it was *his*. Ballydehob's agent had tried to have him evicted — since then, however, the family adopted a quite different policy — a matter of good will —

Never again what had been done

In the year of eighteen eighty-one.

I'll put my little bill in the post. I'm very glad you looked in. I'll just drop a line to the O'Learys to let them know you're on the way. You want to look over the place, I suppose. Travel by Liverpool — more comfortable than Holyhead, though it takes a few hours longer. Good morning.

Exit CROTCHET.

Baker-Fortescue
It is with some trepidation
I embark on this expedition.
It seems there are both bogs and pitfalls
I must put my feet across.
I must keep tight hold of the old kitbag
If I am not to suffer some loss.

Exit BAKER-FORTESCUE.

Enter TERESA *and* SEAMUS (TERESA *is pregnant and nursing a baby*).

Teresa You came home in good time from the fair?
Seamus I did.
Teresa I had thought you would be drinking.
Seamus I would too, for the news that's in it. But it's best you should hear it yourself. Lord Ballydehob is dead.
Teresa Don't we know that already — sure wasn't it in the *Advertiser*?
Seamus Oh it was, but I've confirmed it. I had it quite definite from Tim Hagan at the petrol pump. He died a month since in the London hospitals, there's no doubt about it at all. Now will you listen to me, woman, it's what Tim Hagan's after telling me — it's important, says Hagan. They have not been able to discover the direct heir to the property.
Teresa Lord Ballydehob had a son, surely?
Seamus Ah the title, now, you see, went always with that parcel of land in County Wexford. The bit that's in it here was never entailed. I don't know what that means, but Hagan tell me 'tis a legal loophole for us.
Teresa What d'you mean, a loophole?
Seamus Do you know what I'm after thinking? I think that the lot of it could belong to none other than us.
Teresa Sure it always belonged to us.
Seamus Were there not O'Learys set firm on this ground six hundred years ago when there wasn't an English landlord west of the Shannon?
Teresa You will never get a lawyer to establish you that. Every corner of every paragraph of every law in this country was ravelled up by some Englishman. Our old Irish lawyers and their old Irish books all drowned in the ocean by order of Cromwell, or Queen

Elizabeth, or one of 'em — it's all finished, we can't go back to it.

Seamus Oh can we not? We are a Free State, and very shortly, by all the rumours, about to declare ourselves a Republic. Jasus the minute your man Dev puts that name to his constitution, not a saucer of English law will be left for the cat in the kitchen...

Teresa I hear the postman — he has a letter.

PADRAIC, *as a postman, knocks, and hands her a letter.*

Seamus ...to say nothing of the rats that creep under the back door or the birdeens in their nest in the thick of the thatch — begod, that's not a letter? Who the divel writes a letter to me?

Teresa Crotchet.

Seamus Crotchet — what Crotchet?

Teresa 'Tis Crotchet the lawyer. The ferret.

Seamus From London?

Teresa The ferret that lived ever in the long pocket of Lord Ballydehob's shooting-coat. He has teeth.

Seamus And he says — ?

Teresa He says that the land has passed to a relative.

Seamus To an Englishman, begod.

Teresa To an Honourable, a Baker-Fortescue, lives in Yorkshire...

Seamus Aha, now, that'll be Roderick! Didn't they name him after the bastard evicted my great-grandfather — ho ho boys, we've heard of *him*! A class of a pawnbroker in the streets of Harrogate and a disgrace to a noble house, I remember Hagan telling me —

Teresa That Hagan'd tell you anything. Doesn't he dilute the very petrol from his pump with a pint of paraffin to every gallon?

Seamus If he does so, good luck to him. Thanks be to God I can't afford a motor-car. Nor ever like to, the ways things go.

Teresa So where are we, for all the fine words?

Seamus He says nothing about the Tintawndub. Except he hopes that we will make the Honourable gentleman welcome when he comes. Very likely he's a decent man and will give us no disturbance. Look at that now — here he comes!

Enter BAKER-FORTESCUE, *diffidently, carrying a small suitcase. He walks about quietly, as though sizing up the property.*

Teresa

It would be best to offer up a small prayer, I do think.

Seamus

I am thinking 'twould be better to take hold of a small drink.

He gets a whiskey-bottle and pours himself a glass. BAKER-FORTESCUE *approaches them. They go into a stylised routine of old retainers offering a formal welcome.*

Teresa Ah sure and we're proud to deliver a great welcome to your honour etcetera etcetera...

Aside:

He has teeth the size of gravestones, grin you to powder in a minute
and a half.

Seamus We are honoured and proud, sir, to have your foot upon our
threshold etcetera etcetera...

Aside:

Jasus Mary and Joseph I declare he was expecting it!

Aloud:

Woman, will you pull up a chair. Sure the Honourable gentleman
will take a small drink.

Baker-Fortescue Baker-Fortescue.

Seamus Etcetera.

Teresa Etcetera.

Baker-Fortescue

I had really no idea they were going to be so polite.
Mr Crotchet was quite right.
Can they not be aware of the commercial possibility
Inherent in this traditional antique hospitality?
If they are not, I am: I will turn to account
Their archaic deportment and their Celtic servility:
I will turn it to account and amass a large amount.
I am beginning to think well
Of my neo-colonial estate.
I will keep it. I will not sell.

*All the above, to the audience as he walks about. Now he turns to
the* O'LEARYS:

Good God, it's half-past eight.
I had not thought it was so late.
Very gloomy, is it not, in the bottom of this green valley?
Tell me, how long has my concrete-block Chalet
Remained uninhabited? I was led to believe it was new.
There are hens in its kitchen. I presume they belong to you.
The state of the floor would make my visitors want to spew.

Seamus

The late Lord Ballydehob, sir, always stayed in the hotel.
The convenience of the chickens was a matter of good will.

Teresa

Sir, his lordship had in mind
The Chalet was a mistake and should come down.
Leaving the Tintawndub to stand
As it always stood, upon its own.

You did say — visitors...?

Baker-Fortescue Did I not explain my intentions? Oh I do beg your pardon. I was virtually certain I had made myself clear — I hope I am not already seduced by the mist that does be on the bog —

Seamus The what, sir?

Baker-Fortescue I am absolutely charmed by this little corner of the world, the blue lake, the green glen — much as I should like to, I can't live here all the time. I have a business to attend to in England. But such a well-situated Chalet left vacant for years on end —

Teresa Oh indeed a terrible pity, sir, to have it go to rack and ruin. 'Tis a very strong-built little house.

Seamus (*aside to* TERESA) Does he know that the water from the bank above runs down on a wet day and floods out the front hall?

Teresa (*aside to* SEAMUS) He'd be blind if he hadn't noticed it. But we mention it when he does and not before — keep your wits awake, Seamus — *visitors* — and keep away from that bottle.

Seamus (*aside to* TERESA) Ah sure, just a noggeen — what th'hell d'you mean, *visitors*?

Baker-Fortescue So suitable, do you see, for a quiet untroubled holiday? Say a week or a fortnight at a time, a family-party... You could look after them, could you not?

Seamus A family? Look after who... ?

Teresa (*gesturing at him*) Ss-ssh... Indeed of course we could, sir, and happy to do so, sure the bed-and-breakfast is all the rage these days, why Tim Hagan himself —

Seamus Oh that's it, the tourists — ? Indeed, herself will do the cooking and any gentleman for a day on the lake or a stretch of shooting over the bog —

Baker-Fortescue I can put him safely in your hands.

Teresa There's not a man in Kilnasleeveen with a better notion of the trout and how to attract them —

Seamus Begod, sir, let me give you another glass in your hand. There's a raindrop the size of an egg just fallen smack into that.

Baker-Fortescue I did notice the Chalet has a problem with the wet weather —

Teresa Oh yes sir, indeed it has, Tim Hagan says the porosity of the concrete —

Seamus The porosity of the thatched roof in the Tintawndub, as you see, sir.

Baker-Fortescue Ah, thatch! So little of it left in our English villages, alas, we can't get the craftsmen, you see —

Seamus There's a man above in Kilnasleeveen very good at repairing thatch.

Baker-Fortescue Splendid.

Teresa 'Tis best to renew a thatch every five years —

Seamus Or else with the birds and their nests and the rats and the mice

that's in it and the strong wind — Lord Ballydehob had this one attended to in nineteen thirty-five.

Teresa His lordship was always most considerate.

Baker-Fortescue (*at last looking upwards*)

Five years? The chappie who repaired your thatch
He must indeed have been the best of all good men.
What should have lasted five years he has made endure for ten.
It needs no more than a patch above the door
To extend its rainproof life for at least a score.
What else d'you need to make your home complete?
Do I hear the patter of tiny feet?
A mouse, a rat... ?

Seamus

Five hundred if there's one.

Baker-Fortescue

So get a cat
And then they are dead and gone.
I am putting you in a great way to make money, don't you see —
All you have to do is treat my visitors as you treat me —
For every summer visitor that will bite upon my hook
Five shillings I will give you for your Post Office Savings Book!
And that does not take account of any gratuity
Each visitor will give you of his own generosity —
You have hens, you have cows grazing upon your land,
Your eggs, milk and butter will be in constant demand:
You have heard that in England we have the Era of Austerity —
Enormous sums paid out for the most commonplace commodity:
Eggs and milk and home-made bread
And jam and country butter thickly spread —
Imagine a pound of butter is now worth a pound of gold —

Seamus

We have been told —

Baker-Fortescue (*sings*) [Air: *The Parting Glass*]

'I am the man that brings to you
The secret in the stony ground
Of how the crock of gold beneath
The blackthorn tree is sought and found!'

Seamus (*sings*)

'We'll follow you with shovel and spade
And dig and delve in bog and rock
And drive the little green man away
And wrap our arms around his crock.'

Teresa (*sings*)

'We shall not fear his grin of rage
And all his roars will be in vain —
We have long deserved what we shall get
When we come into our own again — '

Seamus and **Teresa** (*sing*)

'When we come in, when we come in,
When we come into our own again:
O'Leary's house shall not fall down
We shall have no more of grief and pain... '

The refrain is repeated faster and faster; all three have joined hands and spin round in a rapid dance. BAKER-FORTESCUE *breaks it off.*

Baker-Fortescue

You will excuse me if I leave:
My taxi to Limerick Junction and the Dublin train to catch.

The O'LEARYS *continue dancing.* BAKER-FORTESCUE *addresses the audience:*

It would be better if my Chalet were built of stone with a clean thatch.
For my visitors more picturesque and I could charge a higher rent.
I could even call it a castle, people would take it as it was meant...
But I do not want to risk the O'Learys' discontent:
If I thought of swopping them from here to over there
I do not think they'd think I was playing them fair.
My advertisements in the newspapers within two or three days —
Mr O'Leary, the top of the evening — do I have the correct
    phrase... ?

The O'LEARYS *bid him a formalised farewell.*

O'Learys So etcetera, your honour, etcetera etcetera, so...
Baker-Fortescue (*moving away from them*)

But here is a matter that fills me with gloom:
You saw the baby at her bosom
The other within her womb —

Padraic

The other within her womb
Being Padraic O'Leary — me —
In preparation for the tomb.
According to Karl Marx, not one of us can see
What we look at, except
As our class-role may direct.
My eyes at the time being as blind
As the Honourable Fortescue's mind
How could either of us foretell
I was the one he must kill?

THE LAST LEGATEE UNDERSTANDS HIS INHERITANCE
TO BE OF LIMITED ADVANTAGE TO HIM: BUT DETER-
MINES TO MAKE THE BEST OF IT.

Baker-Fortescue

The value of my land is not enhanced, I am afraid.
I had not thought this family would be a family that would breed.
But what can be done?
O'Leary has had his fun
And I must suffer in my pocket for what he did in his damp bed.
In the Irish Free State contraceptives are forbid:
And even if they were not I would still be too late —
I must at any rate dissuade her from conceiving any more:
For if she does by God my property will burst open at wall and floor.
O'Leary gets drunk and his eyes are deeply sunk:
I have reason to speculate his blood will be degenerate.
However, just yet, I need not worry about that.
My advertisement for the papers must at once be written out:
I have a pile of prospective profits to assess and calculate.

Exit BAKER-FORTESCUE.

Teresa

It does not seem to me he intends to renew the roof.

Seamus

And as for his bloody visitors:
When we see them arrive, we will then see the proof.

Exeunt TERESA *and* SEAMUS.

Scene Two

Padraic

The length of time that is past and gone
I shall sum up in a little song.

NINETEEN FIFTY-EIGHT.

He sings, or rather chants, as the metre is irregular:

'So many years for good or ill
The Age of Austerity over the hill
The Tories are in and Labour out —
Private Enterprise runs about
On all four feet like a wolf in the night,
He chops with his teeth at all in sight
The foam runs out at the corner of his jaw
He gulps what he can and howls for more —
Give give give! Let him devour:
He'll burst his belly in half-an-hour... '

Enter BAKER-FORTESCUE.

Baker-Fortescue Oh no he won't, you know — the market is expanding with the resilience of elastic but the margin of safety is both catholic and commodious. The bookings of my Chalet are constant — and at home the old restrictions upon currency exchange, etcetera, have been lifted left and right — such advantage in such matters, such augmentation of export-import — Zurich Zurich Zurich... oh yes, I am alive to it, duplicating, triplicating my Irish prosperity.

Padraic (*sings*)

'Labour is out and the Tories in —

The Suez war we did not win.

High time high time, Macmillan said,

To knock such nonsense on the head.'

Baker-Fortescue Only because they insisted on chickening-out at the last moment. Nasser is a crocodile. Trample him into the mud. Wog!

Padraic (*sings*)

'Pull in our horns, pull in our feet,

Withdraw the cruisers of the Fleet.'

Baker-Fortescue I judged it very wisely at the end of the war when I decided not to remain in government service.

Padraic (*sings*)

'The Americans have a prodigious huge bomb

That can bring the whole world to an end

If we do not do what they tell us to do

We cannot be their little small friend.

They will leave us alone to cry and to groan

Like Anthony Eden with his face to the wall

Who weeps and weeps for the Suez Canal.'

Baker-Fortescue Serve him right. Yellow-belly. Doesn't know where his bread's buttered. Personally I find the Yankees exceedingly civil: provided one remembers their idiosyncracies. Here is a letter I have just received from one of them — a typical satisfied client... !

He reads the letter:

'Kilnasleeveen', she says, 'was the village of our dreams — '

Padraic (*sings*)

'But if we obey and we do as they say

They will feed us with ice-cream and steak every day

They will tuck us up tight in the dark of the night

In an air-conditioned bed with the blankets round your head

And whiter than the white of the White Cliffs of Dover

A pretty little lady to lie under and roll over

So warm and bare and flattering, she whispers in your ear,

'If you don't look out of the window, love,

You have nothing at all to fear... '

Baker-Fortescue 'Animal excrement all over the doorstep, huge tangles of hay filling up the back bedroom — the night of the big wind... ' Odours, she says, noxious odours, fleas and lice from the farmyard... what in God's name has Teresa O'Leary been up to! Mr Crotchet, do you hear me... ?

Enter CROTCHET.

Crotchet Oh yes, I can hear...

Baker-Fortescue Just because Lord Ballydehob let them keep hens in the Chalet when there was nobody there... To whom do they think the property belongs?

Crotchet (*looking through the letter*) They weren't *keeping* the hay in the Chalet, the wind blew it in, it appears...

Baker-Fortescue But Mr Crotchet — *cow-dung*! These people are Americans — from New York! They are terrified of the country-side. She refers further on to 'wild animals' loose in the lane.

Crotchet Dogs?

Baker-Fortescue Bullocks. O'Leary's bullocks. I shall write to his wife.

Crotchet Now be very careful there —

Baker-Fortescue (*taking out pad and preparing to write*) I look to you to advise me if I make a mistake. So: 'My dear Teresa — ' Okay?

Crotchet There is after all no *Mrs* Baker-Fortescue to take umbrage.

Baker-Fortescue Crotchet, I am serious. To continue: 'The letter I have received from Mrs Macnamara is extremely disturbing. If what she says about the fleas and the hay and the cow-dung is true — '

Crotchet No! Give her the benefit of the doubt *before* you put the boot in. A question of psychology.

Baker-Fortescue I see what you mean... 'If what she says about the fleas etcetera is *not* true, then I must know what happened to make her so upset. But, if it *is* true, I can only conclude that for some reason the fence between the Tintawndub and my Chalet is no longer fulfilling its function: I ask myself, how? Can Seamus have possibly taken some of it down to make himself an irregular short-cut? That fence is the legal limit to the activities of your tenancy — '

Crotchet 'Tenancy' — the word is perhaps prejudicial. 'Tenure' might be safer.

Baker-Fortescue Whatever you say. 'In any case it is clear that Mrs Mac-namara feels herself subjected to the worst kind of rural nuisance. Until I am assured that all steps have been taken to prevent its recurrence, I am unable to forward to you your usual gratuity. This will perhaps teach you — '

Crotchet No no no; no sir, no! You are *unable* to forward it. Do not put down on paper you are *penalising* them, for heaven's sake! Let them draw their own conclusions. Now, at once: a change of tone. Revert to your usual agreeable self.

Baker-Fortescue 'Oh, by the way, don't forget, our first guests for the coming year will be Major and Mrs Dreadnought Pole-Hatchet.

The Major is a Member of the Belfast Parliament, and a close
friend of the Prime Minister of Northern Ireland. They will be
arriving for three weeks shortly before Easter. Most important you
protect their privacy against any offensive local demonstrations in
relation to the anniversary of 1916.'

Crotchet You don't think an Ulster Unionist something of a provocation?

Baker-Fortescue

It is not like that these days in the West.
The bitter glue of Irish politics
In that soft climate now no longer sticks.
A Unionist, an Orangeman indeed,
Is seen there as the kind of man they need.
The curdled thunder of his furious drum
He modifies into the industrious hum
Of calculating-machines and clerks with ballpoint pens,
Peers mildly at the world through his bi-focal lens,
And for his only rampart of defence
He finds the ornamental grillwork of his bank
A stronger fortress than the strongest tank.

Padraic He always did.

Baker-Fortescue

In erstwhile hostile Dublin now he frequently may be seen
Taking his lunch-time stroll in Stephen's Green:
Then back to the office, export, import, cash and credit,
The roaring hope of bomb and burst and blood at last is muted —
King Billy and the Pope now both inhabit
The yielding mattress of your Wall Street whore —
A patriotic man like me may well regret
That such is as it is, but we must not forget
Our gore and glory now is doused in an old piss-pot:
The British Empire terrifies no more
With Black-and-Tans and murderous threats of war.

Padraic (*sings*)

'The figures of unemployment
Throughout Ireland increase and increase:
The emigrant ships across the Irish Sea
Heave seasick onwards and do not cease... '

Oh I was to be on one of them: so I know.

Crotchet

You think the North and South are reconciled?

Baker-Fortescue

I know the Irish are no longer wild.

It's obvious, my dear Crotchet, they cannot afford it. Didn't you
tell me so yourself?

*A distant concussion, striking them rigid for a moment of absolute
silence.*

Crotchet

What was that sound
Far over the Northern Irish ground
Was it a bomb? Was it a gun?
Who is that man? I see him run —
An ancient ragged bleeding man
Across the green mountain fast as he can —
He cries aloud from a great wound in his head:

Padraic (*motionless at the back of the stage*)

'Who dares to say the IRA is dead... !'

CROTCHET *and* BAKER-FORTESCUE *look at one another aghast.*

Baker-Fortescue

I do not understand what this should mean...

Padraic

Lie quiet, my love, it was a dreadful dream.
We have them all locked up in a dark box.
It was no man, it was a hunted fox.
Cut off his tail and nail it to your door:
Smear his red blood from ear to ear.
Did I not swear you have no more to fear... ?

Baker-Fortescue Exactly so. Preventive detention both north and south of the Border is most efficiently in force. Mr Crotchet, here is an axiom:

Whether he walk abroad open
Or lie close concealed,
The boldest terrorist in the world
Is not able to thrive
Without the people conspire together
To preserve him alive.

And they certainly don't do that in the Barony of Kilnasleeveen. Decent deferential folk, every one of them, I assure you. So: I'll put this in the post.

While talking he has finished his letter, put it into an envelope, and stamped it. Now he hands it to PADRAIC.

Now: to my luncheon-appointment. Stocks-and-shares, Zurich, the dollar, the drachma, the yen... !

Padraic (*looking at envelope*) This should get to Kilnasleeveen the day after tomorrow.

Exeunt BAKER-FORTESCUE *and* CROTCHET.

Enter TERESA *(pregnant again) and* SEAMUS. PADRAIC *hands* TERESA *the letter. She shows it to* SEAMUS *and opens it.*

Seamus Does he send a postal order?

Teresa He does not. And why would he? The American woman wrote to him a whole scroll of complaints. Didn't I tell you she would?

Seamus (*taking the letter from her*) Fleas, he says, hay, cow-dung — and begod what's all this about his fence? Sure the night of the big wind six yards of that same fence were transported half over the lake and every switch of hay in my stacks distributed between here and Macroom! What the hell will we feed the cattle on till the end of winter, does he say that? Ho ho, 'tis all his fence and the repair and conservation of it, when Tim Hagan dug his posts no more than three inches into the ground for him, sure a field-mouse could thrust it over. Since he sub-let the old petrol-pump and moved into the contracting, that Hagan's truly proved himself a sharp feller for the main chance. I wouldn't care to have the employment of him in the Tintawndub.

Teresa In my opinion, 'tis time we had the employment of somebody.

Seamus Falling down about our ears. But how can we repair our own house, will you tell me that, when the operation of the entire farm has developed into a status of economic disaster?

Teresa And what d'you intend should be done about it, so?

Seamus Ah sure, the old place will last out our lifetime. God knows but we're modest people, we have no great requirement. Though, mind you, if we built a small silo for the cattle-feed...

Teresa The young doctor at the dispensary said it was dangerous for the baby to live any longer here with the cold and the damp that's in it.

Seamus Baby? What baby? Oh Jasus, that's not for another six months.

Teresa Four.

Seamus Jasus, is it four, already? You made a slip in your calculations there, woman, I'm telling you —

Teresa I wonder you're not ashamed.

Seamus Who says I am not ashamed?

Teresa Is it you or myself then that will stand up to the Honourable Baker?

Seamus Stand up to him and do what?

Teresa
Stand up to him and demand
That in our farm upon this land
He shall pay money and he shall take pain
To protect our lives and produce
From the wind and the rain.
Did you say a small silo? He could well afford the cost.
And send him that hospital X-ray of your chest.

Seamus
It would be as well first to get hold of a lawyer.
Let the lawyer then write to him a letter that would be strong:
He writes in his own letters every line of a lawyer —
Why should not a lawyer as well do right as do wrong?
Upon a matter of right this farm is our own.

Teresa

He claims it for himself.

Seamus

Then it is himself that should pay.

Teresa

So let you go to town for a lawyer:
And let you go there today.

Seamus

Tomorrow will be time enough.

Bedamn I would go this minute only for this fierce cough.

Is it catch the bus in this weather? You know well I am not well:
Besides, I am detecting a weakness in my left heel.

Teresa

You have a weakness in your head.

Seamus

I have indeed. 'Tis well-known.

Teresa

Oh 'tis easy to see that nothing will be done.

Seamus

Bedamn I often wonder I don't take to my bed...

And where the hell d'you think you're going?

Teresa I am going into town. Upon your business.

Seamus You have no right to do that. You are the woman of the house and your name is good for nothing at the bottom of a document. A terrible thing when a man can't have obedience beneath his roof... ! I'll tell you what we'll do. I'll go and talk to Tim Hagan. He can put the word out for some of them precast concrete blocks, have a silo begun as soon as the weather lifts up. Sure the Honourable won't know about it till the work is commenced, and by then it'll be too late.

Teresa You're not expecting him to pay?

Seamus If he don't, we put in our ferret, our own lawyer, directly! Or better still, let Hagan do it. If you dropped your man Hagan from a very great height, wouldn't he land with his claws in the neck of the best advocate in Munster?

Teresa But — but — Seamus —

Seamus That's enough. I have me plan, and we stick to it. I'm away to meet Hagan. He'll be in Driscoll's bar, above. Did you ever hear of an American that never complained about anything... ?

Teresa I did not.

Exeunt TERESA *and* SEAMUS, *severally.*

Scene Three

Enter BAKER-FORTESCUE, *reading a letter.*

Baker-Fortescue A most appreciative letter from Major Dreadnought
Pole-Hatchet.

Padraic

EXPOSURE OF THE CONTRADICTIONS OF PARTITION:
WHO GIVES THE ORDERS FOR WHAT, IN WHICH HALF?
NINETEEN FIFTY-NINE.

Baker-Fortescue Mr Crotchet, are you there? 'The fishing was first-rate,
and the people very civil — although of course in Kilnasleeveen
they would be Catholics to a man. How absurd,' he writes, 'to
imagine every Irishman is a furnace of political rage. Except of
course where outside-agitators have made their impact.' Exactly so.
Mr Crotchet — ?

Enter CROTCHET.

Crotchet Oh yes, I can hear...

Baker-Fortescue Major-Dreadnought Pole-Hatchet had an excellent
holiday.

Crotchet Very gratifying, I'm sure.

Baker-Fortescue Or did he? Good God, but just listen to this. 'Only
marred,' he says, 'marred, by the strange odour from the new silo
and the demolition of the gable wall that would have stood between
the Chalet and the prevailing west wind: for this one must thank the
egregious Mr Hagan, who cannot, it appears, put a new roof on a
barn without first removing every wall and fence for two hundred
yards... !'

Crotchet I'm afraid I don't quite understand...

Baker-Fortescue By heaven, sir, but *I* do! 'Mr Hagan,' he continues,
and expects me to receive it as a *joke!*, 'Mr Hagan ought to be
transferred bone-by-bone into the National Museum as a prime
example of "*Contractor Hibernicus Vulgaris Tyrannus* — mid
twentieth-century." ' Does that make it any clearer?

Crotchet "Contractor Hibernicus... " aha, now I follow. Oh dear, my
dear sir, you should never have begun work upon improving that
small-holding without asking my advice.

Baker-Fortescue I have *not* begun work.

Crotchet The consequences, I assure you, are unforseeable, and
infinite...

Baker-Fortescue I tell you, Mr Crotchet, I have not begun work!

Crotchet But you authorised O'Leary —

Baker-Fortescue Oh no, sir, I did not!

Crotchet Are you perfectly certain? There is no letter that could be
quoted against you, no hint, no intimation? You had better let me
see copies of all your correspondence, just in case. But if what you

say is true, you are in quite a strong position.

Baker-Fortescue Position to do what? To pay Hagan a bill for some thousands of pounds? Do you know how much he charged me for putting up that useless fence? And that was work I *did* order — I superintended it in person!

Crotchet But the fence was for the Chalet, not the farmyard? You yourself have made no improvements to the Tintawndub, is that not so?

Baker-Fortescue I myself have charged them no *rent* for the Tintawndub! As you told me, the position of the O'Learys is so very — non-committal — extra-constitutional — ah, outside the established framework.

Crotchet Rather like the Irish Free State, as it then was. I mean, within the British Empire, and yet —

Baker-Fortescue A very good friend of mine in Bomber Command, 1943, had to make a forced landing in County Kildare. D'you know, the bloody buggers tried to have him interned! In a camp full of Oberleutnants out of U-boats, if you please. But as I understand it, the Irish Free State was the result of a treaty worked out with Lloyd George when I was no more than a schoolboy. It imposed upon the Irish a number of responsibilities they have signally failed to live up to. This has not been the case with my property, Mr Crotchet. There can be absolutely no doubt that the Tintawndub belongs to *me*. You have the deeds, have you not? If the O'Learys misconduct themselves, I can turn them out: and I shall.

Crotchet But you don't want them out.

Baker-Fortescue Not at present, certainly not. They are essential to the proper administration of my holiday-chalet. But in due course, if I can discover a more — a more *loyal* set of dependants, the law, even the Irish law, I am confident, will be on my side.

Crotchet I am not altogether so sure.

Baker-Fortescue But the deeds, documents, papers — I have the *papers*, Mr Crotchet!

Crotchet Which do not define O'Leary. You need at least one more document, to *confirm* him in his place.

Baker-Fortescue I don't *want* to confirm him! I want it to be possible to —

Crotchet If need be, to turn the family out. You can't have that until you know exactly upon what terms he is there. He won't live very much longer, but —

An old man of the sea
With his legs around your throat
And *after* him his weeping widow
And his children, and no doubt
His children's children also and their wives —
Have you not thought
How long and how far this inordinate rout

Of uncontrollable hunger will chase
And outface and disgrace
You to the rim of your grave... ?

You may wish to develop the property at some future date — for
example, an hotel. You may wish yourself to get married: you will
need to leave an unencumbered inheritance to your son.

Baker-Fortescue

Yes yes, but do not forget
Any document for O'Leary
Must be agreed by O'Leary:
The Irish Free State
Was agreed by solemn treaty —
And repudiated at a late date.
They pronounced themselves cheated
And formed a Republic.

Crotchet

And yet in the end they were measurably defeated.

They laid claim to a Republic of 32 Counties; they are compelled to
make do with no more than 26.

Baker-Fortescue Mr Crotchet, you are confusing me...

Crotchet Oh no, I'm not: I am drawing a significant analogy, which I'm
quite sure you can grasp — *if* you have a mind that is jumping and
leaping like mine.

Baker-Fortescue But I haven't, and I don't pretend to have. I am a simple business man, not a ballet-dancer. I leave the slyboot bits to
you: and I expect you to explain 'em to me, damn your eyes, in
black and white.

Crotchet Yes, yes, indeed you do, yes. You are in fact becoming rather
stupid, are you not, when confronted by my dialectical agility?

Baker-Fortescue There's no need to be insolent. You first of all intimidate me by telling me that generations of these damned
O'Learys will be squatting on my land forever if something is not
done: and then when I ask you to —

Crotchet Intimidated... confused... stupid... and yet you began with
straightforward righteous anger and a most justified grievance.
Don't you see — there is a pattern? And if I were your antagonist
instead of your friend, what could I not now do to embroil you to
your own ruin? Psychology, my dear sir. You can do just the same
yourself.

Baker-Fortescue Ah... ?

Crotchet Ah... you take the point? You need to get O'Leary to agree to
a document that will not be to the ultimate advantage of his family.
He is filled with righteous anger: he is a simple farmer, just as you
are a simple business man: you must therefore be his ballet-dancer.
To return to my analogy: Lloyd George made a treaty with Michael
Collins which to be sure Michael Collins would never have agreed

to had he understood the implications. In black and white: the Irish leader was intimidated, and confused, and in the end made thoroughly stupid. He brought back to Dublin for his pains the ruin of his Republican ideal.

Baker-Fortescue But, if you are asking me to trick O'Leary out of his rights —

Crotchet Alleged rights —

Baker-Fortescue Of course, of course — alleged — goes without saying —

Crotchet No it don't.

Baker-Fortescue Surely, Mr Crotchet, this would be very far from the proper thing?

Crotchet I think you are confounding morality with legality.

He sings: [Air: *Pretty Polly Perkins*]

'Intelligent application of the process of Law
Is available to all without favour or fear:
Is available to all who can meet the small bill
Of a first-rate solicitor with hearty good will!'

Padraic (*sings*)

'Toodle-oo toodle-oo toodle-oodle oo doo
If the Law plays its tricks, let it play them for *you*!'

Crotchet (*sings*)

'The process of Law is Doe versus Roe
If one of them will stay then the other must go:
If one of them will fall then the other must stand
All you need is the right bit of paper in hand.'

Padraic (*sings*)

'Toodle-oo toodle-oo toodle-oodle oo doo
If the Law plays its tricks, let it play them for *you*!'

Baker-Fortescue (*sings*)

'The process of Law can be long or be short
But a claim more established in broad open court
Is established for ever and any attempt
To impugn its morality is denounced as contempt.'

Padraic (*sings*)

'Toodle-oo toodle-oo toodle-oodle oo doo
If the Law plays its tricks, let it play them for *you*!'

Baker-Fortescue (*sings*)

'The concept of *trickery* is quite out of place — '

Crotchet (*sings*)

'The word you should use, sir, is *Legal Device*:
The opposite party being equally aware — '

Baker-Fortescue (*sings*)

'If he don't get in first, he will not get his share!'

Padraic (*sings*)

'Toodle-oo toodle-oo toodle-oodle oo *dee*
If a man is not blind, it's assumed he can see — '

Crotchet (*sings*)
> 'If a man is not deaf, it's assumed he can hear — '

Baker-Fortescue (*sings*)
> 'If a man is not barmy, it's assumed he has wit — '

Exeunt CROTCHET *and* BAKER-FORTESCUE, *dancing.*

Padraic (*sings*)
> 'O'Leary O'Leary the challenge is clear:
> Come up to the struggle and prove yourself fit!'

> Because already your proud contender is once more launched upon the tide!

BAKER-FORTESCUE *enters with a small suitcase, and stands around helplessly.*

Baker-Fortescue (*calling*) Mrs O'Leary! O'Leary!... Seamus!... Teresa! Where are you? You, boy, I see you, yes you, over there, don't try to hide from me — who are you? Patrick, is it? Pad-ray-ic? Pat! Pat O'Leary, come here, boy, you know me — Paddy, damn you — here!

Padraic (*off the edge of the stage, as a small boy*) Oh Mr Baker, Mr Fortescue, 'tis yourself... !

Baker-Fortescue Of course it is myself.

Padraic (*at side of stage, to audience*) 'Twas himself. What would I know of the situation with my father, only for the telegram that had come to put the heart across him and drove him to Driscoll's like a mad dog.

Baker-Fortescue Did he not get my telegram — your father — where is he?

Padraic (*as a small boy*) I think, sir, he will be beyond...

He disappears, and then reappears unnoticed.

Baker-Fortescue The Chalet's locked up, the farmhouse is locked up. And good God, look at my gooseberry bushes!

Enter HAGAN.

Hagan I'm sorry, sir, about them bushes — we had no choice in the matter —

Baker-Fortescue Eh? What... ? Oh, Hagan. I fancy you have some explaining to do, Mr Hagan, have you not?

Hagan Oh indeed, sir, a question of attaining the top of the cowshed roof. I had to put me ladder somewhere. The gooseberry patch was the only place where —

Baker-Fortescue And in my Chalet? The broken windows?

Hagan Ah: 'twas the same ladder: to manoeuvre it, d'you see, between the pigsty and the Chalet, where the wall of the one is adjacent to the —

Baker-Fortescue Mr Hagan, from whom, might I ask, do you receive payment?

Hagan The job was authorised, sir, by Seamus O'Leary himself.

Baker-Fortescue And who is Seamus O'Leary to authorise —

Hagan In his capacity as your agent for the property and the up-keep.

Baker-Fortescue Who told you he was my agent?

Hagan Why, you yourself did, sir. You have always referred to him so.

Baker-Fortescue Now look here, Hagan: do you have my signature for this work or do you not?

Hagan It has always been the custom in this part of the world, sir, when the landlord is an absentee, that the agent should be delegated to —

Baker-Fortescue I assure you, Mr Hagan, you will not make that stand up in court before a Judge.

Hagan Oh I wouldn't be so sure: local custom in these parts is a very powerful word.

Baker-Fortescue All work upon this site will cease forthwith, Mr Hagan.

Hagan Whatever you say, sir. Good night to you, so.

Baker-Fortescue One moment. Where's O'Leary?

Hagan (*hands him a paper*) I think he will be beyond. Just the invoice for the building blocks and timber...

BAKER-FORTESCUE *crumples the document furiously and throws it back.*

Hagan (*sings*) [Air: *Chevy Chase*]
'Your honour dear, this was not wise.
Tim Hagan's a crafty lad:
And an enemy of great venom
If you choose to fight him at all... '

Padraic (*sings*)
'Remember his business interests
By politics are reinforced —
He's a climbing lad and a grasping lad
And a power in the Fianna Fail!'

Baker-Fortescue In the what?

Hagan Ah wouldn't you know, like an Englishman always, he pretends he doesn't know.

Exit HAGAN.

Padraic

THE LAST OF THE IMPERIALISTS CONFRONTS FACE-TO-FACE THE LAST OF THE SONS OF THE SOIL.

The O'LEARYS *enter.* SEAMUS *nervously tries to hide behind* TERESA *when he sees* BAKER-FORTESCUE. TERESA *is pregnant again.*

Baker-Fortescue Ah, Mrs O'Leary, an unexpected pleasure!

Teresa Oh your honour, why didn't you give the notice you were coming?

Baker-Fortescue I suppose the Post Office does not deliver telegrams?

Aside to audience:

Good God I declare the woman
Is about to litter again!

To TERESA, *taking her aside:*

Mrs O'Leary, I do warn you: this is not wise.
Do you want a child born that cannot open its eyes,
With a red hole instead of a backbone
And one-third of a living brain?

Teresa

Oh God help us what kind of a devil
Would put words in your mouth like that!

Baker-Fortescue

Mrs O'Leary, I do warn you:
Your husband is not fit.
Unanimous medical opinion has consistently laid down
That a man of your husband's habits
And his weaknesses — all well-known —
Cannot without danger be permitted to procreate.
I find it most unfortunate it should happen on my estate.

Teresa I cannot believe I have heard what you have said.

SEAMUS *comes over to them.*

Seamus — he said to me —

Seamus Between meself and the Honourable there is an issue of principle.
I would ask you to leave us alone.

Teresa Are you sure that you know what you're doing? Perhaps tomorrow — ?

Seamus Today.

Teresa I know *I* am in no condition to speak reasonably to that man.

Exit TERESA.

Seamus Now sir: to transact business. An explanation, if you please?

Baker-Fortescue I came here, Mr O'Leary, to obtain an explanation
from *you*! By what right have you given orders —

Seamus — for the improvement of the Tintawndub? I will answer you
that when you answer me this. Who's is it, yours or mine?

Baker-Fortescue You live in it, certainly. I am the owner.

Seamus If you are, you have the obligation to see it is kept in repair. If
you refuse then 'tis clear you concede that the rights of the property
appertain to meself.

Baker-Fortescue Now look here, O'Leary, I have not hitherto charged
you one penny of rent for this small-holding, but —

Seamus You have not. And why not?

Baker-Fortescue Because —

Seamus Because you knew you did not dare, the foul condition it was in! But the minute you see improvements — ho ho how the man's brain turns round in avarice at the escalation of the value! 'Tis the same tale we have been told in Munster for three hundred years — the poor man's roof is worth nothing till he makes it worth something: and every particle of that worth is directly diverted to the strong-box of the landlord. And what benefit has the landlord put into the land — by construction, by muscular toil, by the hump of his shoulders or the blistering of his skin? Bedamn you do not even *live* here — if you look over the place for one week in twelve months we are to consider ourselves honoured! Oh you pass with some diligence your fragments of paper from the head-office of one bank to the head-office of the other: and by the time you draw them out again, by the same token they are converted into the fat goose upon your table and the cabbage and roast potatoes and the gravy poured over it. I tell you truth, me bold and honourable: all that I have said to you, I have writ down upon this paper.

He takes a document from his pocket.

O'Leary is not deceived: nor will he be intimidated.

Baker-Fortescue My dear sir, I have no intention of deceiving you, or intimidating you. There has cleary been a most unfortunate failure of communication here. Will you not sit down quietly like a reasonable man, and help me sort it all out?

Padraic

I was not there when Seamus took the sword
And dagger of his own unaided word
Aloft in trembling fingers holding true
Our ancient right of life in face of Fortescue.
I was not there: but I bear in mind the tale
Of how another Irish champion, brave and afraid
At the one same time, just like my father, made
His own defiance. They said afterwards, that he too failed...
Nineteen hundred and twenty-one, years upon years of hate —
Michael Collins with the bold Lloyd George
Sat down to sort it out.
Said Michael Collins to the bold Lloyd George —

Seamus (*as Collins*)

We have you beat both black and blue.

Padraic

Said the bold Lloyd George to Michael Collins —

Baker-Fortescue (*as Lloyd George*)

The next move is up to you.
You have driven us demented with your murderous IRA
The whole map is besmothered with blood.
We can fight and fight, and fight for ever —
But to whom will be the good?

You have been an enemy: you can be a friend:
Dear sir, let us make an end.
Lay down your terms and we shall meet them
With a free and generous hand.

SEAMUS *passes him the paper.*

But first of all we must not neglect
The hospitality of London town,
Whole-hearted admiration
Of the entire British nation
For your courage and determination
Such honour and respect —

He pockets the paper.

I'll look this over, let my ministers decide
Just how much we can give you and how soon.

BAKER-FORTESCUE *retires.*

Padraic

It has been said
Brave Collins got most beastly drunk.
This was not true.
It has been said
Brave Collins found his head
So turned by adulation
That he knew not what to do...

Seamus (*as Collins*)

Responsibility, not liquor, compels my brain
Like a wild insane electric train
Around around around — around —
Where will it *stop...* !

BAKER-FORTESCUE *comes in again behind him.*

Baker-Fortescue Now, Mr O'Leary, shall we get down to brass-tacks? You see, Mr O'Leary, the situation is this: as you told Timothy Hagan, you are my agent in Kilnasleeveen: the protection of my property depends upon you. You do realise, by the way, that you yourself have no protection... ? I mean, security in your work, in the powers vested in you as my accredited representative here. It's a heavy responsibility when I am so often away.

Seamus An onerous bloody burden, so it is, so it is.

Baker-Fortescue It has been pointed out to me, that in fairness to yourself and family, your position in the Tintawndub here, your security of tenure, your right to the responsibility you so ably carry out, should be regularised and correctly registered...

He passes SEAMUS *a paper.*

Padraic
Said Michael Collins to the bold Lloyd George —
Seamus (*as Collins, examining the paper*)
This is not the same document as the one I gave you.
Padraic
Said the bold Lloyd George to Michael Collins —
Baker-Fortescue (*as Lloyd George*)
Certain amendments for your own security:
Here and there... one or two...
Padraic
Said Collins with the red fire on his cheek —
Seamus (*as Collins*)
You think that you are strong and I am weak —
Baker-Fortescue (*as Lloyd George*)
So strong, my friend, that if you do not agree,
Immediate terrible war will be set free
Across the whole of Ireland, nothing you've known so far
From torturing Tans or hangmen shall compare
With that huge avalanche of horror I can rear
Above the mountain-slopes of your deceitful nation
Now, even now, before the sunset of this very day... !
Seamus (*as himself, suddenly broken*) Oh Mr Baker, sir, all I want, sir, is to enjoy for the rest of my life the rightful roof above my house, sir, my own house, sir, my wife and family, my bit of land —

Yet you tell me you'd turn me out to beg my way
Lie down in a ditch to starve and die
The same as my great-grandfather... My God I never thought
A decent English gentleman would do me such great hurt.
Baker-Fortescue Oh dear, my dear Seamus, you have most totally mis-understood. I mean, supposing, my dear fellow, I were to be killed in a motor-accident, someone else would inherit the property, and that someone else, as things stand, could indeed evict you: and without redress! You must not be put at risk.
Seamus Risk — ? Begod — no — ! Evict me, is it? Let any man try that and I swear I'll have his blood!
Baker-Fortescue No no, sir, not his blood. His legal power, that is sufficient. And there is the defensive weapon by which it can be achieved.

He indicates the paper. SEAMUS *studies it.*

Padraic They called in a couple of the neighbours to be the witnesses. And he read the paper, right through. And it was explained to him.
Baker-Fortescue You do understand, don't you — this gives you exactly what you told me you want — your rightful roof, yours, for the rest of your life...

SEAMUS *signs the document.*

Padraic This is a Life-tenancy Agreement between the Honourable Roderick Baker-Fortescue and Seamus O'Leary Esquire. According to its terms the said Seamus O'Leary receives absolute entitlement to reside for the term of his natural life in the small-holding known as 'The Tintawndub' appertaining to the property known as 'The Chalet, Kilnasleeveen', said small-holding being absolutely the freehold property of the said Baker-Fortescue. Rent to be paid: nil. County-rate, and water-rate, where applicable, to be paid by the freeholder. The freeholder undertakes to keep said Tintawndub and all appertenances and messuages in good and sufficient repair at all times. Upon decease of said O'Leary, tenure of said Tintawndub reverts at will to the freeholder. That's it.

And that is that
And that is all.
If John Doe is to stand
Then Richard Roe must fall.

During the above speech, BAKER-FORTESCUE *has turned his back on* SEAMUS *and the audience.* SEAMUS *slowly subsides to the ground.*

Baker-Fortescue Before I return to Harrogate, a brief letter to the man Hagan — leave it in at the local Post Office — I don't want to have words with him personally.

Writing a postcard.

'Resume work upon *cowshed* alone: complete it as soon as possible.' He won't like it, but I am reducing the scale of his operations. He is only to do about half what he had hoped to do.

Exit BAKER-FORTESCUE.

Enter TERESA.

Teresa What has he done to him? And what has he made him do?

PADRAIC *shows her the signed document.*

He has put his name to *that*?

She sings: [Air: *The Red-haired Man's Wife*]

'Oh shame upon Seamus O'Leary,
What have you agreed?
You've handed over your land and your house
Without any need:
Your wife and your children,
Your life you have given away

For a portion of paper
Like the pay that's the wage of a slave.

You are weak, you are sick,
A mere wreck of a man on the ground:
Alive you will never rise up
If you cannot stand now.
The children who loved you
Must break and forsake you and go
Far over the ocean
From the home that their father has sold.

It is not as though
The police and the bailiffs arrived
With bludgeons and rifles
To drive us all out in the night —
We'd have then had our pride
We could fight them and maybe we'd win:
What pride in a man
With one smile and one threat he gives in?'

Seamus (*struggling to his knees*) Oh God forgive me, Teresa, dear God, what should we do? For a start, we do this...

He strikes a match and burns the document.

It never happened, so. It is forgot.

Teresa It is remembered: and by himself: at the time when we least shall want it.

She leads him away.

Padraic And that is the end of the first half of the story — the first half of *my* story. But because, as you have seen, it was outside of my control, I daresay you'd do best to think of it as the Prologue. That was it.

Exit.

ACT TWO
Scene One

Enter PADRAIC, *as a living man.*

Padraic

NINETEEN SIXTY-EIGHT

He sings: He sings: [Air: *The Wearing of the Green*]

'From the year of nineteen fifty-nine
To nineteen sixty-eight
The fat men of the fat half-world
Had food on every plate.

The lean men of the naked world
Grew leaner every day
And if they put their faces up
Their teeth were kicked away:

And if they dared to link their arms
Or set their shoulders wide
Such furious dogs were flung on them
They bled both back and side.

And if in narrow holes they crouched
Defences to contrive,
They were smeared with flaming jelly
Till not one was left alive.

For the fat men at their dinner-board
Could never bear to think
That creeping fingers from below
Might steal their meal and drink.'

Seamus O'Leary my father so suddenly dead in the Regional Hospital, for nine years now he was bent and bowed over like the limb of a mountain thorn: alternate breath he coughed up blood: Monday and Tuesday he would have died upon the spot: Wednesday and Thurday he put his boots among the turf and would dig for his living and cough: Friday and Saturday he would crouch by the fire in Driscoll's Bar and his glass would never be empty: Sunday he would obey his duty, he'd uncover his head just inside the church-door: and Monday once again he would have died upon the spot. Who the hell could dance attendance on a man that went from us as slow and as tiresome as that? Me mother's telegram came to Manchester where I worked as a bricklayer: God knows she could not tell I had travelled that week to Dunfermline. He had but the one son: and three days late for the funeral. Already fallen down on my first responsibility... But begod I'll make up for it.

Enter HAGAN. PADRAIC *stands apart, his back turned, meditating.*

Hagan So he comes home, the son and heir, three days late. Fat men thin men, is it? Would you call *me* fat? Because if I am, then he's thin, and I don't care for the sound of such comparisons in Kilnasleeveen. Ah, Padraic — there ye are: I'm sorry for your trouble, son. Oh indeed, that's the grave. As you see there's no stone ordered yet. But you'll be wanting to sort out the debit and credit before you'd think of that.

Padraic I haven't had a sight of the will. But the Tintawndub —

Hagan Will be left to you of course. Would you think it worth the working, that bit o'land now, I very much doubt it. In the heel of the hunt you'd be advised to look out for a class of a job, that is if you mean to stay here. I could always use a bricklayer, part-time. Think it over.

Padraic I haven't decided whether to stay or go back.

Hagan Maybe after all you'd do best to go back, take the old lady with you and your sister Siobhan, why not?

Padraic What would happen to the Tintawndub?

Hagan Sure you'd always find a purchaser. Would you care for a jar at Driscoll's?

Padraic Ah no, I must get home. I promised I wouldn't be long.

Hagan Good luck to you, so...

Exit PADRAIC.

Hagan 'What would happen to the Tintawndub... ?' They've told him nothing of the state of affairs. Life-tenancy Agreement — ha! When he finds out, there'll be ructions: and Tim Hagan is now established as the sympathetic friend and compassionate counsellor.

I am, you see, a business man
I look for the main chance where I can.
Creeping fingers from below?
I smudge 'em out like flakes of snow... !

Exit HAGAN.

Enter SIOBHAN.

Padraic Here's Siobhan, my youngest sister, the only one not yet married or gone into a convent: something's to be done for her directly, but what? You're still determined, are you, to carry on through the college till you qualify as a physiotherapist or whatever? But to support you out of three fields and a leaky old half-rebuilt farmhouse, and all my work and contacts away over in England, it's not good sense. Why don't you and mammy come over with me as soon as we can get the Tintawndub sold? There's not only colleges in England, there's the welfare state, government grants — together with the money we get out of the sale — and on my own account I'm doing well enough there to organise a permanent home for you both.

Siobhan Money out of the sale? You're not trying to tell me Hagan has made you an offer?

Padraic He seemed to be edging towards it.

Siobhan Nonsense, Paudeen, how can he have been? He knows as well as we do that you can't sell the farm so long as the ownership is in dispute.

Padraic Dispute? Who disputes it?

Siobhan Harrogate, the Honourable Baker, who do you think?

Padraic Ah no, he owns the Chalet, the Tintawndub was always ours. Baker-Fortescue never had a leg to stand on in that matter — sure, if he owned it, wouldn't we always have paid him rent?

Siobhan I don't know: but I do know he claims it, all fifteen acres. So we can't sell. And what's more, we can't leave. As long as we stay put we are asserting our own claim, and there's nothing he can do except what he's always done — let us live here and work the farm. There's no reason at all why I shouldn't learn to follow my professional career in my own country these days: the time is long past an educated woman had to look towards England for a living. But if need be I'd give up the college for a year to set things on a sound footing. But I certainly won't quit just to please some British businessman who thinks that no-one in Ireland has a right to their own life. Anyway, mammy won't leave under any circumstances, I may tell you: so that's that.

Padraic Sentimental idealism confounded with short-sighted economic confusion. High time we were rid of it.

Siobhan High time we were rid of your Manchester fashion of talk. Denouncing everyone left and right out of a pocket-full of English pamphlets, and you've only been home a few hours.

Padraic That's right, I'm a stranger in this bloody place, I've been away since I was seventeen, I'm no sooner back than everything you say to me makes me want to get out again as quick as I can —

Enter TERESA.

Teresa Get out, did you say? Isn't that exactly what the man wants! But we're not going to give it to him, oh no... unless of course you were to sell under his feet so quiet and quick he would never know a thing about it till after it was done. Do you think that could be possible — perhaps a quiet word with Tim Hagan... ?

Padraic It's not likely, it's a legal question — we'd have to have some sort of document about the ownership —

Teresa Ah — document — is it papers? No, Paudeen, oh no, no more o' them! Thank you very much indeed —

Padraic What d'you mean, no *more* of 'em?

Teresa Never mind, he'll do nothing, so long as we're here, it's *ours* —

Enter HAGAN.

Hagan

SENTIMENTAL IDEALISM CONFOUNDED WITH SHORT-SIGHTED ECONOMIC CONFUSION.

Through the post comes a letter with an evil report.
Her hand takes the letter, the trap springs, the mice are caught.

He gives a letter to TERESA *and exit.*

Teresa Paudeen, I can't read it. It is from him: there is poison, deadly poison in his words. The last child of all I should have brought forth into the world was born dead, for no other reason than the curse of this — this gentleman he spoke over me while I was carrying her. Paudeen, read the letter.

Padraic (*having taken the letter*) He says, he is sorry to hear of the death. He says, 'You do realise that the Life-Tenancy I afforded Seamus must necessarily expire at — at the same time that he did...'! If this means what I think it means we have not even got the right to stay put on the land and make any sort of claim on that basis. All the generations we have been here and none of it worth anything! What else does he say? He might have allowed you to stay on here, he says — except that he had heard you had 'entertained offers from certain business interests to dispose of what was not yours...'?

Teresa Sure Hagan and some others of them were speaking about our selling the farm, but —

Padraic 'Reluctantly therefore... left with no alternative... reluctantly put the Life-Tenancy Agreement in the hands of my solicitor... instructions to terminate forthwith. Rod. Baker-Fortescue, H.O.N. in brackets.'

Siobhan He wants us all off the land this minute: and no recompense at all?

Padraic If we don't go, he'll go to court and get the court to put the sheriff in, and evict us — oh he has that power. Oh God what the devil was in this Agreement? Do we not have a copy of it?

Siobhan (*taking letter and looking at it*)
And this is the letter that he writes to be read
By the side of the death-bed
Of the man who did aid his interest year in and year out
Like an ass between the shafts of an over-loaded cart.

Teresa Lord Ballydehob always said the historical right, the moral right, he always put it, was our own, and he never insisted we —

Padraic Moral... historical... there is no right in Ireland but the right of
the English Law carried over from the old days. Yet dammit we do
have a Constitution in this country, maintains as a basic principle
the integrity of the Irish family and all the children of the nation. It
must surely prevent a man signing over every right of his own
children to some capitalist across the water —

Siobhan Then if that's so we meet him head on in the courts and fight
the case right down to the end.

Teresa That's it: we're not budging.

Siobhan We're not budging.

Teresa Oh now that it's too late I see the whole thing so very clear — the
straddle of his great boots and the mud and blood that stains them —

Padraic Boots, mud...?

Teresa

Oh 'tis apparent.
'Tis the man with the long purse
Spreads his feet across this land
His boots that leave no room for the tread of anyone else:
He opens his purse and dips in his hand,
Pulls it out again tight-clenched
Being full to the bend of his thumb:
And those few for whom he opens it
Are the same few every time.

Siobhan Tim Hagan for one.

Teresa

Oh well indeed for himself
Tim Hagan has done.
And yet nothing more
Than what was begun
When the Harrogate Honourable
Came to us out of the war
And bought your father like a slave
Body and soul and all alive.
And now in the end he has killed him dead
And he hangs his great red blade
Hard over your mother's head.

Padraic

You shall not go.
This home is your own
And you are to remain.
There is nothing I shall not dare
To make sure that you do.

Teresa

Padraic, you are young.
But you are my one son
I put my trust in you.

Exit TERESA.

Padraic Ah for God's sake a bit of courage comes easy to anyone — the bloody practicality'll finish *me* before I'm started. Have we no legal papers whatever? Do we know any lawyers?

Siobhan Do you think if he takes us to court and we don't have the papers we will lose?

Padraic I don't know, but a court-case would stir up the politics —

Siobhan You mean, barricade the Tintawndub like the days of Parnell? Put the posters up all over the country — 'No Brit Evictions in Kilnasleeveen!' — you mean that?

Padraic Not quite. I mean Mass Support and the Solidarity of the Working Class —

Siobhan Oh Manchester talk — fairy-tales — your English trade unions —

Padraic

The very opposite to Parnell.

Parnell is not the name

I would summon for this game:

Trade unions to Parnell

Were very devils out of hell.

Trade unions would have fallen under condemnation and black ban

Had the government ever passed into the power of that proud man.

To put it bluntly, Siobhan, he would have sold out the Revolution.

Siobhan Look, Paudeen, we have had the Revolution in Ireland.

Padraic 1916 I suppose...?

Ah Jesus in that glorious year

What did they do at all?

Shot to death James Connolly

Propped up against a wall.

And those greedy men whom all his life

He had fought till he could not stand

Had the whole of the Irish nation

Delivered into their hand.

Siobhan Let you talk about your Socialism, you'll be denounced by the priest. But if, on the other hand, we had the priest on our side —

Padraic Did you talk to him?

Siobhan I think mammy did. 'The Law must take its course,' he said. Where do the clergy live but at the bottom of the long purse?.

Padraic

There must be *something* in this land —

Not to find it out, pick it up,

Just like that, out of hand —

But never will I credit

That the people's dreams of power

Justice, dignity, at last

Are rising up on every shore
Except the one that *we* inhabit — !
Parnell, and the delusive past —
Manchester-talk, oh yes, like withered winter grass:
You laugh at the one and I sneer at the other.
But sister and sister, brother and brother —
We are the people and the land belongs to *us*!

Enter HAGAN.

Hagan (*to audience*)
They are standing all alone
And their words are blown away:
How *can* the land belong to them — ?
They can talk they can talk
But we know they cannot pay...

SIOBHAN *and* PADRAIC *are going out.* HAGAN *catches* PADRAIC*'s eye and makes a covert sign. Mistrustfully* PADRAIC *lets his sister go on alone and joins* HAGAN.

Hagan Now I heard something at Driscoll's about your Harrogate man and his pretensions. Wouldn't you know the cute bugger'd be after holding the closest card up his sleeve the whole time? Does your mother intend to fight it in the courts?

Padraic She does.

Hagan Ah... she won't win. Not a chance. But it's bound to take a long time and it's bound to arouse a deal of popular feeling. Now you want to be building on that. And you want to make friends with a few certain people — name no names but you take my meaning — they'll be able to look after you if and when things come to the worst.

Enter MULHOLLAND. *He had a poster reading: 'Land League and Small Farmers' Civil Rights. Public Meeting Sunday 12.30'. He also carries a paste-pot and brush.*

Ah — Terry Mulholland!

Mulholland Tim Hagan, the very man. You'll put a couple of these up for us on your building-yard gateposts, sure you will —

He hands HAGAN *one or two posters.*

Hagan This is Padraic O'Leary, you'll have heard about his trouble — the Tintawndub, you know what I mean. I'll leave you with him, so.

MULHOLLAND *greets* PADRAIC *and gets into earnest talk with him.* HAGAN, *downstage, looks at the posters with distaste.*

Hagan (*to audience*) Public meeting — a sight *too* public, that's not the way at all — there's no need at all to disseminate this class of nonsense. I thought they were supposed to be an *illegal* organisation... ? People should stay where they belong, or we're all of us disordered.

He crumples the posters and goes out.

Mulholland (*continuing his remarks to Padraic*) Keep clear of that Hagan — calls himself a Republican, but that's only for show. He's no more interested in civil rights or democracy than any other gombeen business chancer — it's men like him helped De Valera send the genuine Republicans into gaol as soon as the Brits put the screws on. I was interned myself for seven years, so I know what I'm talking about. I'm a qualified school-teacher, but damn the job I've been able to find since the day they let me out. I get expenses from the Republican Movement for organising things for them in these parts, and otherwise I live on the dole. So you see, when I tell you that Civil Rights is the one struggle worth fighting for in all Ireland north and south, you'll understand I speak from experience.

Padraic And how does that affect me in regard to this eviction?

Mulholland If you join the movement, come to the meetings, make a few speeches for us, you'd find that this apparently minor affair of a ratty little Brit landlord, with a single bit of paper to force an Irish family out of their home onto the road, is a straight indication of all that's wrong with this country — the ownership of the Six Counties, the subjection of the Fianna Fail government to multi-national industrial syndicates, the Offences Against The State Act, internment for Republicans, the lot.

Padraic You want to use me for your party advantage?

Mulholland Aren't you an Irishman? The Republican Movement is for the advantage of all oppressed people in Ireland: and you don't need me to tell you that the greater the agitation, the greater the pressures on the courts when your case comes to trial. It could even be that your mother's predicament becomes so notorious that they won't dare give a verdict in favour of the Harrogate man. None of the other political outfits in the country could do that for you, bet your boots. Ah... is it the physical-force secret-society side of the thing makes you twist your face at me? Oh it does, you've been mixing with your left-wing crowd in England who'd make out that all nationalism is directly opposed to socialism. But that's only because they have no experience of the colonial situation, except for all the benefits it's brought them over the years. But the bombing and shooting's a virtual dead letter these days — though the likes of Tim Hagan still hope to make use of it. What we're concerned about now is solid organisation to expose the economic contradictions.

Padraic That makes sense.

Mulholland I thought you'd think so.

Padraic My sister would even call it Manchester talk.

Mulholland Only because she's forgotten what Wolfe Tone had to say in 1798 — 'the people of no property' — his link with the French Revolution — remember, our republican roots are far deeper grounded in the true hunger of the people than any of your British chauvinist marxism. Come to Driscoll's and we'll talk about it...

Exeunt. (As he speaks, he has been pasting up one of his posters at the back of the stage).

Re-enter HAGAN. *He mutilates the poster.*

Hagan

SENTIMENTAL IDEALISM CONFOUNDED WITH BLOODY SUBVERSION.

And not only in Kilnasleeveen.

Scene Two

Hagan

NINETEEN SIXTY-EIGHT: OCTOBER

Exit HAGAN.

Enter CROTCHET, *followed by* BAKER-FORTESCUE.

Crotchet What the devil is going on in Londonderry these days? Just caught it on the television. Battering and bloodshed. It could have repercussions! I must take immediate steps... my stockbroker...

He goes over the telephone and dials a number.

Mr Giltedge? Good morning. Crotchet here. Now listen, my shares in Harland and Wolff of Belfast. I want you to get rid of them, sell them... that's right, and put the money in — ah — South African Mining stock, got that?... Oh, Giltedge, you still there? My friend Mr Baker-Fortescue would like you to do the same for him... Yes yes, very good, good-bye, my dear fellow.

He rings off.

He says he will do it for you. One must act in good time.

PADRAIC *and* MULHOLLAND *appear at the rear as a chorus*

Padraic *and* **Mulholland** (*sing*) [Air: *The Boys of Wexford*]
>'Beneath the walls of Derry town
>They marched with banners high
>"One man one vote" and "civil rights"
>United was the cry.'

Baker-Fortescue Thank you, thank you...

Crotchet Barbarous, isn't it?

Baker-Fortescue The police there, of course, are allowed very free rein, most necessary, I believe.

Padraic *and* **Mulholland** (*sing*)
>'They bore no arms, they threatened none
>As they marched beneath that wall:
>But the RUC with bloody glee
>On the people were let fall.
>
>They did not care whom they struck down
>In their rage so blind and wild:
>Old mens' gray hair they did not spare
>Nor the mother with her child.'

Baker-Fortescue Disgracefully exaggerated: but even were it true I would thoroughly approve. We have had quiet and good order in that part of the United Kingdom for nearly fifty years. If anyone wants to dispute the fact he most certainly should not do so by assembling large crowds and indulging in emotional oratory.

Crotchet That sort of thing can only lead to violence: and it is very good to see that the police are determined that no violence shall take place.

Padraic *and* **Mulholland** (*sing*)
>'Let the men of Stormont tremble now
>At the work they have begun
>For by the blow that they have struck
>Their power is all undone.
>
>The blood they shed in Derry town
>On the pavement let it lie.
>Till Ireland's free from north to south
>Those pools will not be dry,'

PADRAIC *and* MULHOLLAND *withdraw.*

Crotchet Yes... from north, to south, yes? Do I detect a faint suggestion that *no* part of Ireland is free? You know what that means, don't you? Those agitators over there are not green any longer, but —

Baker-Fortescue Not green?

Crotchet Red.

Baker-Fortescue But — but — surely not in Kilnasleeveen...?

Crotchet Yes... Concerning Kilnasleeveen: I am one hundred per cent certain that the Irish court will give us the possession order we are asking for. But, what d'you propose to do with the Tintawndub once she's out of it?

Baker-Fortescue I think I shall probably sell it. Hagan is interested, you know. There have been other enquiries as well. My partner has a contact in Blackpool with a notion of developing the entire site — continental holiday-village, yachting, you know, girls in bikinis — I suppose the O'Leary woman has asked for compensation?

Crotchet Her solicitors have put forward the figure of £5,000.

Baker-Fortescue Good God, whatever for?

Crotchet For the improvements that they paid for themselves. I offered seven hundred and fifty. It might keep us out of a contested court-case, you see. Ticklish.

Baker-Fortescue Rubbish: and five hundred would have been more than enough!

Exit BAKER-FORTESCUE.

Crotchet I do beg your pardon, I'm sure...

Re-enter BAKER-FORTESCUE.

Baker-Fortescue No — Crotchet — one moment — you said '*red*'? Civil rights for Catholics is a *communist* demand... ? What religion is Teresa O'Leary? I have just had a letter from Timothy Hagan: he writes —

HAGAN *appears at the back as* BAKER-FORTESCUE *shows* CROTCHET *the letter.*

Hagan 'I have kept him as I told you under my eye in my own employ: but only that they know I will tolerate no trade-unions, he'd make more trouble with my other men than his presence is worth. All his talk about Manchester and some powerful great building-site strike he helped organise there last year.'

Baker-Fortescue D'you see what I mean — red, Crotchet — *red*!

Hagan 'He's also been involved in certain secret political meetings, d'you know what I mean. Most distasteful in the view of the large Dutch and German interests in the tourist business in these parts. In regard to which my offer for the Tintawndub still stands...'

HAGAN *withdraws.*

Baker-Fortescue Appalling how fast this perversion can spread! In 1967 it was students in Berlin, earlier this year it was students and just about everyone else in Paris — today it is Londonderry — to-morrow... telephone!

He goes to telephone, looking up a number in his pocketbook: he dials.

Ministry of Defence? Extension 8967000. Hello... hello: I wish to speak to Wing-Commander Black, if he is with you...

To CROTCHET:

I suppose we are secure? This line is not equipped with a scrambler, I notice.

Into phone:

Ah: Wing-Commander Black? I am right to call you 'Black'? Same code-name as of old?... Yes yes, of course, we're not scrambled, must be careful, security... You do know who this is, I take it?... Not? Then suppose I remind you of another and less official sobriquet by which you were once known? Ha ha — 'Dogsballock!' You remember — in a jeep outside the burgomaster's office in Wuppertal, just after the Hun had surrendered, with the wife of the Untergruppenführer under arrest in the back seat... Yes, yes, indeed it is, it is Roddy Baker-F!...

To CROTCHET.

Of course he remembers, he's an incredibly well-trained man.

Into phone:

Now, Dogsballock, look here — the current situation in the Province of Ulster... Yes yes I know that at the moment it is only the concern of the civil police. But let us not deceive ourselves: no more than a matter of months before the armed forces of the Crown are involved there up to the hilt! Before they involve *them*, they are bound to involve *you*, can't bring in the troops without help from the Old Firm, eh?... There is no need to be discourteous, I am only endeavouring to help! I will continue, if you permit. A representative of the Stormont Government has already identified the so-called civil rights campaign as nothing more than a front for the IRA. And the IRA he has identified as a front for international C-O-M-M-U-N-I-S-M and we all know what *that* is. At least, *I* do: I hope *you* do: I mean, that's what you're paid for. Now: I have no doubt that you will already have considered the probability of IRA bases of support and supply being established south of the border to maintain the subversion in the north. The question is, where?... Dogsballock, I am this very moment giving you the answer! Kilnasleeveen — four syllables, and crammed to the brim with a priest-ridden malignant mob of — of damnable defaulters, evaders of rent, and squatters upon property to which they have absolutely not a shadow of title! I just thought I'd let you know... I also thought an officer as highly placed as you are in the occult milieu of military intelligence would be a little more forthcoming when an old — as you might say — associate condescends to volunteer some information. You always were an unwholesome little tick: and I am bitterly sorry I remembered your telephone number. You behaved like a perfect cad that evening in Wuppertal: and Penelope thought so too.

He rings off.

Yet he is, as I said, a highly-trained man — he'll not forget what I've told him.

Crotchet Who's Penelope?

Baker-Fortescue I do not propose to bandy a lady's name with you. You have your instructions, Mr Attorney — carry on!

Exeunt severally.

Scene Three

Enter PADRAIC, *dressed as a building worker, with appropriate gear which he carries across the stage as though engaged on a job.* HAGAN *is with him giving various instructions in dumb-show. They pass across the stage, then* HAGAN *leaves.* PADRAIC *hurriedly pastes up a poster reading 'No Brit Evictions: Mass Meeting! Saturday' He goes out again.* HAGAN *re-enters and tears part of the poster down.*

Hagan

NINETEEN SEVENTY: MINORITY AGITATION BECOMES A MAJORITY THREAT.

Exit HAGAN.

Enter LIMEGRAVE *festooned with cameras.*

During this scene PADRAIC *moves about at the back, at work and oblivious. At one point he replaces the torn poster.*

Limegrave
Old Wingco Black, my chief, is said
To be already failing in his head.
The Secret Service falls on evil days —
He is too old, although he once was wise:
Against the Hun, the Red, the Chinaman, the Wog,
He did good service once: but what a fog
Comes down upon his mind from this Hibernian bog...!
Because the streets of Derry run with blood,
To Munster I am sent: and for what good?

He takes a rice-paper document from a false heel in his shoe.

He says: 'Kilnasleeveen: take a cottage, make use of an appropriate cover.' No problem, my normal work, genuine and unbreakable: I make documentary films for BBC2. Ecology and conservation. The best-known perhaps would be *The Sloblands of Shannon*, with soundtrack composed by a traditional tinker from Antrim who plays the tin whistle. Enough of that — *business.* 'Prepare a report upon subject already known to Special Branch, Manchester: O'Leary, Padraic: we have the files, trouble-making trade-union militant, political overtones. Suggest examine links with Republican Movement.' I have. Deeply implicated. Small Farmers' Land League, Civil Rights for Offshore Fishermen, demonstrations against pollution outside multinational chemical-works, Limerick. So much trouble in the North: *West* of Ireland at all costs must be kept quiet. 'Subject may well form nucleus of an undesirable element.' Thank you, Wingco Black! O'Leary's little sister is very far from undesirable. According to routine procedure I have begun my surveillance there: nearest approach to subject himself, so far, long-distance photography. Oh: I was supposed to have got rid of this upon arrival. So easy to forget, when women are confusing the trail...

He begins to eat his orders.

SIOBHAN *has entered behind him.*

Siobhan If that is chewing-gum, can I have a piece?

Limegrave My love, you are late. No, chewing-gum — no. A local herb, I'd have thought you'd have known about it — St Brigid's Eyelash, traditional remedy for arthritis — does your mother not use it?

Siobhan If she has a pain she takes an aspirin.

Limegrave Oh no she must try this, let me pick you a bunch...

He is trying to kiss her.

Siobhan You won't find any round my neck. I thought you would be filming the mosses and fern at the lakeside. Well, here you are, amongst them. Get out your old light-metre.

Limegrave Not even BBC2 wants the mosses and fern uninhabited. Sit down and display yourself, and unwind three or four layers of wool.

He starts to pose her, and attempts to remove her scarf. She prevents him unfastening anything further.

Siobhan Mr Limegrave, do you know my brother? He is working just above: the new bungalow this side of the bohereen.

Limegrave Oh he is, is he? Crafty colleen, you are protected, dear oh dear...

Aside to audience:

Little does she know it was with full deliberation
I persuaded her to meet me in this very secluded place.
I want a good close-up of the militant brother's face:
We do not have one in our file.

To SIOBHAN:

So: there we are: your back to the bushes — and smile!

PADRAIC, *in the midst of his work, stops and watches them for a moment.* LIMEGRAVE *is taking movie-film, chiefly of Siobhan, but includes a shot of Padraic.* PADRAIC, *unaware of this, goes away again.* LIMEGRAVE *speaks to the audience:*

Out-of-focus, imperfect, zoom-lens on the bloody blink:
Draw him in that little bit closer — how to do it — let me think...

To SIOBHAN:

Dreadfully ugly bungalow, don't you agree? Environmental disaster if ever I saw one.

Siobhan Let me tell you there is nothing more important than decent houses in Kilnasleeveen! That bungalow would be God's gift to my mother if only she could afford it.

Limegrave Oh I know I know I know — evicted by the Brits — you will never be anything other than a terrible little Fenian —

Siobhan
Tourist oh tourist, you come and you go:
You talk and you talk, there is nothing you do not know.
Is there nothing you can talk about you really understand?
What is that in your hand?

Limegrave (*who has been picking flowers*) Snowdrops for a necklace for the whitest neck in the Emerald Isle. One thing I would talk about, I do understand —

Siobhan So what is it, Mr Limegrave?

Limegrave
Dear God, my name is Julian, how often must it be said?
I just want to get the measurement
Of the circumference of your sweet head...
I just want to talk about you, and about me:
We met by chance on a lonely road
In a gap of the broken weather,
Do we continue our journey apart and alone:
Or do we travel together...?

Siobhan I don't think I want to commit myself to anything like that.

PADRAIC *has come nearer.* LIMEGRAVE *finds he has not enough flowers and goes aside to look for some more.* PADRAIC *comes*

down to his sister. During the next passage of dialogue
LIMEGRAVE *succeeds in getting his close-up shots.*

Padraic For Christ's sake I've been watching you for half the afternoon. I don't know who the hell that bloody man is, but he's not one of us. You should leave him alone.

Siobhan I have told you who he is. He is an Englishman and he's here to make films.

Padraic Exactly the same class as that bastard Baker-Fortescue.

Siobhan He is not: he is an artist!

Padraic One quarter of him may be: the rest is export-import, an exploiter in two words. Get rid of him.

Siobhan I will not.

Padraic Or at least confront him with the situation we are in: put his wonderful artistry to some test of the truth.

LIMEGRAVE *rejoins them.*

Limegrave Oh... Hello... You must be —

Siobhan This is my brother. Paudeen, I want you to meet Mr Limegrave.

Limegrave Julian, please. How d'you do? Your sister has told me a good deal about you.

Padraic Did she tell you we are fighting an eviction from an absentee British landlord?

Limegrave Yes, she did mention it, most unfortunate business.

Padraic And have you any suggestions as to what we should do?

Limegrave Ah — a good solicitor...?

Padraic Pointless. We have had one: the case drags on and on.

There is but the one way that I can see at all:
Why wouldn't the IRA put a bomb under his block-concrete wall?

Limegrave Dear oh dear, do we need to bring *violence* into it?

Padraic Eviction is bloody violence! Will you look at the Six Counties and what your British Army's doing up there!

Limegrave Surely, to keep the peace, protect Catholics against the Protestants...

Padraic My God, but he *believes* it! So: Mr Englishman, settle the eviction without violence.

Limegrave Can I ask you a straight question? Are you in any way connected with any branch of the IRA?

Padraic And if I were, d'you think I'd bloody tell you? If I thought that they could help us, I'd join 'em like a shot. As it is, I put my trust in the recipes of Lenin.

Limegrave Lenin? Oh dear oh dear...

Padraic 'Educate, Agitate, Organise', was the precept of your man. And that's what we are doing in Kilnasleeveen at this moment.

Limegrave Have you had much response?

Padraic Kilnasleeveen, Mr Englishman, is a suburb of the Falls Road!

Exit PADRAIC.

Limegrave He talks in such slogans. You've a tendency that way yourself. It could get you into trouble.

PADRAIC *suddenly comes back again.*

Padraic What the hell do you mean by that!

Limegrave Oh look here, my dear chap, I didn't mean anything...

Padraic Sure I know you upside-down. Siobhan, begod, I know him, and I know him upside-down. Anything that anyone says that is *meant*, is a subversion of the status-quo! Siobhan, he has failed the test!

Limegrave Test...?

Padraic When all is said, I take one look at you: you're just bloody inconsiderable — I'd insult myself by regarding you as a factor in our business. Siobhan, you know the score: your consciousness of this man is determined by his class-role!

Exit PADRAIC.

Limegrave (*waiting carefully till he has gone*) You see, slogans: he's still at it... Too bourgeois perhaps if I put this round your neck?

He offers her the garland.

Siobhan It would not: but I think it would be taking a bit too much for granted. I have to go up to the shops before they close.

Limegrave Ah. I'll come with you.

Siobhan I don't think that would be a very good idea.

Exit SIOBHAN.

Limegrave Now I think of it, neither do I. Still, I shall see her again. And then we shall see...

I am looking for a dead body in a heap of rotten manure.

He detaches one flower from the garland and looks at it.

I find it: and I find a single snowdrop growing there.
Its roots have been put down into the dead man's breast
Deep-groping in the gangrened gash that was the cause of death:
I cannot move the corpse unless I break the flower:
To take it out and cherish it is not within my power.

He presses the flower to a pulp between his fingers and drops it. He then realises he is still holding the rest of the garland. He looks at it at arm's length. BUTLER McREEK *comes in and takes hold of the end of it, so that they are holding it up between them. A pause.*

Butler McReek Mr Julian Limegrave?

Limegrave Oh yes, good afternoon. How do you do?

Butler McReek Butler McReek. I had heard you were living amongst us. So, a bit belatedly, welcome to Kilnasleeveen. You're making a film they tell me. We have a great country here for the creative contemplation. If you're walking in the direction of Driscoll's...?

Limegrave That's very kind.

Butler McReek I don't in fact live here. A Dubliner, in point of fact. A class of an architect, by way of a trade. I take occasion now and again to put the odd notion of a speculation into the briefcase of a good friend. The tourism, now. Possibilities of a holiday village; now we're in the EEC a scheme like that'd fill many a decent man's bucket. You wouldn't be considering a stake in such a thing yourself?

Limegrave I don't think so.

Butler McReek Aha, you're the cautious man! Would I be wrong now to suppose your careful demeanour suggests you are a fisherman?

Limegrave I hope to do a little while I am here.

Butler McReek Ah, you'll need a good ghillie — I mean someone to explain to you the relative value of each separate trout. There's many in this lake are scarcely worth the length of your line, especially if you're hoping to — ah — market your catch in London. Most of *my* clients, of course, are to be found, rather, in — ah —

Limegrave Dublin...

Aside:

Dublin Castle, Special Branch. I knew it as soon as he spoke to me. Wingco Black thought they would very soon be in contact.

Butler McReek Where are you going?

Limegrave You said something about a drink at Driscoll's.

Butler McReek So damn crowded in Driscoll's... one question before we get there. Do you have precise *instructions* to confabulate with the Ould McReek: and are you just a cowboy playing your own game and damn the locals?

Limegrave Look here, old man, don't you think you're a little bit too direct?

Butler McReek Jesus Christ, I've made an abrasion on his self-protective English skin. If you want to be a tortoise, be a tortoise, goddammit. But I've had *my* instructions. They say, the full honours of our Irish hospitality... Driscoll's?

Limegrave Driscoll's.

Exeunt.

Scene Four

Enter HAGAN.

Hagan

THE RASH REPUDIATION OF THE TRADITIONAL GUAR-
DIANS OF THE OPPRESSED REAPS ITS OWN REWARD:
NINETEEN SEVENTY-ONE.

Agitate, educate, let the people organise,
Open their eyes, take stock, get wise —
Won't they look upon me and my legitimate enterprise
From an altogether different view?
Kilnasleeveen, Tim Hagan, will have seen the last of *you.*

MULHOLLAND, *followed by* PADRAIC, *comes in. They have their
arms full of posters, which they start to paste up, advertising 'Small
Farmers' Rally and March': 'Civil Rights on the Land': 'Nationalise
the Land Now': 'March against Foreign Landlords': 'No
Evictions': 'Tillage or Tourism, the People's Choice', etc.* HAGAN
gestures towards MULHOLLAND:

Now that feller, passing through the place twice a year with his
begrudging pamphlets, is no danger to anyone, unless and until he
slaps his mildew into the groin of a young man with a legitimate
grievance who is determined to remain here and bloody *root*
himself — will you look at him, fouling the ground between his feet
with the effluvium of irrational protest. Ahoy there, Terence,
d'you mind now if I borrow your young activist a moment?

Mulholland (*humourously to Padraic*) I think the wage-slave is wanted
by the expropriator — I'll finish the work...

PADRAIC *comes over to* HAGAN.

Hagan (*to* PADRAIC) Look, the owner of that damn bungalow's
behind in his payment, so from tomorrow you're off the job and
I'm putting you instead to the repair of Matty Driscoll's roof...

He looks at one of the posters:

Yet another weekend on the street? 'Tis the burning ideal, I suppose, will carry you through. I wouldn't have the feet for it.

Padraic The Land Commission is permitting sound arable to be taken
over for a motel on the road to the coast. Here's the leaflet.

Hagan Fair enough, 'tis a good cause. And how much has that same
motel to do with the Tintawndub?

Padraic We must view it in the proper perspective. Domination of the land by extra-territorial financial-political interests —

Hagan Of course of course of course, and 'tis best solved in the one way. Direct action against bricks-and-mortar. Why the hell doesn't the Movement put a bomb under the motel once it's built? By the same token, Baker-Fortescue. It's three years since your mother began wasting time and good money in that eedjit of a court-case — adjournment upon adjournment, and appeals I wouldn't wonder to the throne of the Pope himself — would you want me to drop the hint for you — just a word in your man's ear...?

He indicates MULHOLLAND.

You may be too nervous to mention it yourself, sure you don't have the tradition, being so long away in England...

Padraic What's in it for you? I mean damnit, you're Fianna Fail, the personal manifestation in Kilnasleeveen of Jack Lynch himself. Wouldn't you say the IRA is a bit of a threat to *you*?

Hagan
You are not as discerning as I had expected.
Don't you know that Tim Hagan has a great care to be protected?

Padraic As far as I am concerned we have an overt political programme and that's the only way to get anywhere.

He turns his back on HAGAN *and goes to help again with the posters.*

Exit HAGAN.

Mulholland Now that he's gone, I've a piece of news for you. I had a message from Dublin. They're expecting internment to be introduced any day now in the North. The Movement's badly up against it there, and the Provos splitting away from us hasn't helped at all. We look to be losing half our strength in one swoop unless we're careful: and even if we are careful we have nothing like the men on the ground that we need if we're to hold our own. They're sending me to Belfast — at least, off and on — more of a liaison job than a permanent posting, but I shan't be able to give much serious attention to affairs in these parts any more. Good God, and to think I told you physical force was a dead letter? Civil rights — overt politics — the enlightened British public gave a short answer to that notion.

Padraic British Army, you mean.

Mulholland And who turned the Army onto the Nationalist people three days after the British public put Ted Heath into Downing Street? Do we say 'God forgive them for they know not what they do'? Or, equally, 'God look after them for *we* know what they'll get!' Mind you, I'm not so daft as to believe that that Labour Party of theirs would have done any different in the long run.

Padraic Just sufficient of an eedjit to have *hoped* for it, that's all.

They laugh.

Mulholland Here, how did you come by that cut on your forehead?

Padraic A drunk in Driscoll's yard — ran against me with a bottle when I'm after taking a leak. I think he was put up to it.

Mulholland I'd say he was paid to do it. There are times when intimidation can only be defeated by the same thing in reverse.

Padraic Ah, sure, but intimidate *who*? If you're to go north, what's to happen down here?

Mulholland Ah: there's the difficulty. Affairs in Kilnasleeveen, from now on, are peripheral. And I am deputed to inform you, official from the Executive, that they are left in your charge.

Padraic What — all of it? The bloody eviction — and — and — this?

Mulholland I shan't be away till we've had the march and rally. But you do realise the motel is a foregone conclusion: and so, I am sorry to say, is the result of your mother's lawsuit. What we call a one-off issue. Irrelevant to the main campaign in the west.

Padraic I thought they *were* the main campaign.

Mulholland Not any more. Redefined by the Executive. Direct all future effort among rank-and-file trade-unionists in the new industrial development around the urban population centres. That ought to suit you — it's what you did in England, and begod it's what you're good at.

Padraic I'm not leaving the eviction to take care of itself — damn it, Terry, it's my own home — I shall have to take action!

Mulholland Then you must take it unsupported by the Movement outside of this area.

Padraic If I have to, I will. All right, a foregone conclusion. My mother loses her court-case and they come to force her out of the farm. I'll fill the bloody farm with trade-unionists from your urban centres — civil rights and sit-down protest and 'We-will-not-be-moved' — I know these factory-workers, they know me, I've more than enough contacts built up with 'em by now: if the Executive don't like it, they can lump it, that's all! I think before we're done they'll be having to send a few Ulstermen down here to do your liaison job in reverse, so they will! We don't need the British Army to show us where the enemy is. And by the same token, Terry, no more is the motel a foregone conclusion either. I happen to know that the planning permission has not yet been obtained!

Enter HAGAN.

Hagan (*to audience*) Ah, no: he's wrong there. The County Manager already put the word out in private. It won't be official till next week when the contract is awarded. Guess who to...

He takes MULHOLLAND *aside.*

D'you mind if I have a word. About this Chalet and the Harrogate export-import. Incompetent placing of gelignite produces nothing more than a broken window.

Mulholland Is that a fact?

Hagan When I see the British Army in the North let loose upon the Catholic people like a horde of bloody Balubas, I bear in mind that I am more than a contractor for putting up buildings, I am frequently paid for demolishing them as well. I demand a true Irishman's right to make myself useful.

Mulholland Don't tell me — tell him. He's in charge from now on.

He indicates PADRAIC.

Hagan (*most disconcerted*) What's that?

Padraic (*coming over to them*) Tell him what?

Mulholland Oh, just to let you know that if an agent provocateur is what you need around the place, who better than himself to supply it? Keep the faith.

Exit MULHOLLAND.

Hagan (*grimly*) I don't think you need trouble yourself to turn up on any of my contracts any more. Sure your smallholding and its care and maintenance will take all of your time from now on.

Padraic It'll take all of the time of this complacent community from now on, I'll tell you that! We're neither leaving it, nor selling it, nor bloody blowing it down: so work out where you stand, my friend, in relation to the wrath to come!

Exit PADRAIC. HAGAN *commences to mutilate some of the posters.*

Hagan

Oh begod but it will come:
Maybe not from just where you think.
A bare-faced beggar the like o'that
Telling Hagan to swim or to sink...!
Oh no, it is not his homestead
Needs now to be blown down,
But himself in short order.
By no-one from this town —

We don't want to create too much of a scandal. The best way's to prepare the way with a small word to the Parish Priest — denunciation from the pulpit for atheist agitation — and then — the next developments...

Enter BUTLER McREEK *and* LIMEGRAVE.

Indicates BUTLER McREEK:

And here in the nick of time arrives the first of them, with his broad portfolio. Mr Butler McReek, a short word...

To LIMEGRAVE:

Good evening, sir, fine day...

To BUTLER McREEK, *confidentially:*

That feller we're after talking about, you know what I mean — Manchester... oh 'tis worse now than ever it was. I have it absolutely certain he has infiltrated the IRA with a proposal for explosive sabotage of all foreign-owned property between here and the banks of Shannon, if the Honourable's possession order is turned down by the courts. Now you know there's a certain Senator with his £20,000 holiday-villa below at the mouth of the waterfall — why, he rang me up this morning, oh fearful of disturbances — he says, 'Hagan, what the hell goes on...?'

To himself, checking over some money.

I have a fiver for the Priest, he's collecting for a new confessional...

He is about to go out, but BUTLER McREEK *stops him.*

Butler McReek For God's sake get on to your man in Dublin — find out about the bloody court-case!

HAGAN *nods and goes over to the telephone.*

Limegrave He said 'absolutely certain'?

Butler McReek Does it tie in or doesn't it with what O'Leary said to you about bombs under block-concrete walls? What time did you say you would be calling for Miss O'Leary?

Limegrave Half-past six. The film begins at eight.

Butler McReek (*looking at his watch*) Six o'clock on the dot. She's not home yet: the old woman's gone out: himself is in the Tintawndub alone. Let you knock upon the door then and we will see what there is to be seen.

LIMEGRAVE *knocks. Enter* PADRAIC.

Limegrave Hello, Padraic, there you are. Is Siobhan at home yet?

Padraic (*grumpily, but accepting the Limegrave relationship*) Oh, you're to take her to the pictures of course. You'd best come in. Sit down and wait for her. Would you want a cup o'tea — or something...?

Limegrave That would be splendid.

Butler McReek The cup o'tea would do us fine... or maybe — *something* — if you have that...

PADRAIC *goes out.*

Padraic (*from off-stage*) Milk or sugar?

Limegrave No milk — a slice of lemon.

Padraic (*off*) Slice of what?

Butler McReek When exactly is the date for your mother's appearance in court?

Padraic (*off*) Twenty-third of next month.

Butler McReek (*aside*) If she wins it, she is safe in the ould homestead for ever and thank God there'll be no function left for me in Kilnaslee-veen. Where the devil is Tim Hagan, he could ha' made that call ten times over...?

Hagan (*at telephone*) Godsake, girl, I said *Dublin*! You've put me through to Ballyjamesduff and me last fivepenny piece has got stuck in the sodding slot!

PADRAIC *comes in with cups of tea.*

Butler McReek (*to* PADRAIC) I wonder now with your politics, you wouldn't have looked for political help in this case. Sure the whole set-up is neo-colonial, I'd ha' thought that you Socialists —

Limegrave *International* Socialists, old man. Trade-union backing? The Labour Party even?

Butler McReek The *Irish* Labour Party — go out on a limb to help a capitalist peasant-proprietor? Or maybe you had in mind the British connection — TUC from over the sea! Ah no, we've to look at this as an anachronistic aspect of our unsolved insoluble national question, what?

Padraic (*in a sudden outburst*) Which outside of the Republican Move-ment is of no interest whatever to working-class organisations anywhere! Internationalism of the working-class — as far as we go, it means nothing but do as you're told by the Brits — because begod didn't they *invent* it! Tolpuddle and Peterloo...! Good God, we want you *out* of here — we do *not* require advice as to how best to retain your influence in the most painless proletarian form!

Limegrave That's very strong.

Butler McReek The heartfelt utterance of the authentic Republican Croppy: mark and learn it, Mr Englishman, there's a death-knell in every syllable.

LIMEGRAVE *chokes in his tea.*

Padraic (*apologetically*) Ah never mind, but I'm half-distracted trying to dig up the cash for these lawyers. I banked everything on a high price for our Connemara ponies: but no good.

Butler McReek Ponies... I wonder... Have you thought of Enniskillen?

Padraic I have not.

Butler McReek There is a fair at Enniskillen on — let me see — the thir-teenth. I heard tell of a man called Pole-Hatchet is searching high and low for the genuine western ponies — he has a notable stud up there — he exports to America.

Padraic Is it Dreadnought Pole-Hatchet? Sure we know about him — he stayed in the Chalet one time.

Butler McReek He's the man you want to see. You'll get no better price in Ireland.

Hagan (*at telephone*) Is the Minister not there?... In the House for a division, is he? Well, his Personal Private Secretary — ah, Mr Foley, good evening to you, sir. This is Hagan, from Kilnasleeveen. I was ringing to enquire, oh entirely confidentially, about this application by the Honourable Baker-Fortescue, his property here... Aha, yes. Jasus, 'tis just as I thought. Will ye pass on to the Minister I consider myself free to take whatever local action appears best. Good-night, sir, I'm more than grateful.

He rings off. BUTLER McREEK, *having noticed him talking, has crept up behind him.* HAGAN *draws him into a corner, and whispers.*

'Tis as I thought. A fixed job. They have a Fianna Fail judge put up to take the case and he's bound to decide in favour of the Honourable. They're aware there'll be local ructions: but the Minister is very keen on a Riviera-type holiday village to be built on the lakeshore, and he's confident that any subversion can be *contained*. D'ye see what I mean...?

They both look at PADRAIC.

In regard to the holiday-village — how long will it take you to get the plans drawn up?

Butler McReek (*taking papers out of his portfolio*) I have a rough class of a sketch-design already prepared for you. It will involve the demolition of both the farm-buildings and the Chalet... You know: I don't think we ought to be looking at this here. Fold it up into your pocket, man, have some sense!

Hagan Ah security, yes indeed: when the Minister himself has enough money in it to sink Noah's Ark.

Butler McReek At any rate, we go ahead. Julian: we go ahead.

HAGAN *withdraws.*

Enter SIOBHAN.

So I'll leave you to your motion-picture.

Exit BUTLER McREEK.

Limegrave Oh... Siobhan. It's damned awkward, but I can't make it tonight, as a matter of fact I'm going back to England first thing tomorrow morning.

Siobhan Tomorrow? Why so soon?

Limegrave The truth is, I think I've done all I can do here.

Exit LIMEGRAVE.

Siobhan (*sings*) [Air: *The Streets of Laredo*]

    'Oh why would I think that he might have stayed longer

    Oh why would I think that he might have delayed?

    Our trouble is our own and he cannot be sharing it:

    And the dark of our evening is the dawn of his day.'

Padraic To get the ponies to Enniskillen, I must acquire a class of a van. I wonder would Tim Hagan let me have the use of his?

Hagan (*coming forward again*) He would, boy, he would. She's a grand ould yoke for the road.

Siobhan Enniskillen?

Padraic The ponies.

Siobhan (*alarmed*) But you'll have to cross the Border.

Padraic Thousands do it every week.

Siobhan Paudeen, for God's sake, take care of yourself, so.

Exit SIOBHAN.

HAGAN *retires.*

Padraic

    Care of myself — what care?

    What have I to do there

    But make use of the Six Counties, accept Partition

    For the sake, for God's sake, of the O'Leary family fortune?

    Baker-Fortescue can in no wise be destroyed upon his own:

    So where do I go, what do I join?

    In the end do I take up the traditional Republican gun

    Or pay heed to Mulholland and break every nerve in my brain

    Attempting to organise unorganised ignorant women and men —

    Impossible choice of two horns, unbridged since 1916:

    So many so courageous have fallen down dead in between.

In the meanwhile, get rid of these ponies.

He sings: [Air: *The Black Horse*]

'On the thirteenth day of August in nineteen seventy-one

I took a load of horseflesh up to Enniskillen town.

The sun was bright and the grass was green and the western wind did blow:

Not careless nor light-heartedly along that road I drove.'

Nonetheless in the wide quiet landscape all the turmoil in my mind became ridiculous, out of proportion.

He sings:

'I did not think until too late of what had taken place — '

Hagan (*coming forward, singing*)

' — That on the ninth of August many men had met their fate:

Internment was determined on, half Belfast was on fire.
Throughout the North the torturers gave vent to their cruel desire.'

Padraic (*sings*)
'In the middle of that bloody week three ponies I had sold
To a certain Orange officer who filled my purse with gold:
I turned my empty van around and for home I did set forth.
May God destroy the day on which I entered in the North!'

Enter BUTLER McREEK *and goes to the telephone: he dials.*

Butler McReek Royal Ulster Constabulary, Enniskillen? Special Operations? Thank you... Inspector? Butler McReek, Kilnasleeveen. Mr Limegrave's young friend has gone to the fair. A large red horsebox, *Hagan and Son Contractor*, number NZM 432. You have that?... You'll pass it on.

He rings off and exit.

Hagan (*sings*)
'On the road towards the Border out of Enniskillen town
You go five miles, you go six miles, the road goes up and down,
There's a hump-back bridge and a twisted bend like the leg of a
    broken dog:
They have blocked the road with a barb-wire coil that is nailed to a
    twelve-inch log.'

Exit HAGAN.

Sound of a van approaching at speed. Twin headlights illuminate the stage. Brakes screech and van heard to come to a stop. The CORPORAL *is picked out in the headlights. He carries a submachine gun.*

Corporal Switch off them lights and get out of that truck! Come on, come on, move it!

The headlights go out. Another light is now cast on the stage from a powerful handlamp carried by the PRIVATE. PADRAIC *comes in from behind the source of the headlights.*

Right, let's be having you!
Private Driving licence, insurance, customs clearance, come on —
Corporal Come on, let's be having you!

PADRAIC *fumbles with the documents. The* CORPORAL *snatches them and riffles them through.*

Name?
Padraic I — O'Leary — I — ah —
Corporal Can't hear you!
Padraic I said —
Corporal Vehicle number — come on, your fucken number!

Padraic Jesus, I can't tell you — it's gone out of my head —

Private (*over by the van*) NZM 432.

Corporal That's it. We take him in.

Padraic But I —

Corporal Don't you *but* me, you bastard Fenian murderer!

Padraic I'm here to sell my ponies and that's all —

Corporal And I'm here to sell *myself* — I'm what you lot call a mercenary. To make my wife a fucken widow because the fucken Irish have all gone mad. An't you found his fucken gun yet?

Private (*who has been searching Padraic*) He ent got one.

Corporal Ent he? He fucken will, by he gets to the barracks. MOVE!

They run PADRAIC *savagely off the stage.*

Enter INTELLIGENCE OFFICER.

Intelligence Officer Erroneous to believe that interrogation-in-depth involves simply a process of uncontrolled brutality. We recognise the violent terrorist is a mentally-sick person. Our methods are therapeutic. If you like, a branch of the Medical Services. I myself have been trained as a doctor and am subject accordingly to the Hippocratic Oath. We know already that this man is a member of the Official IRA. In that capacity he becomes one of my patients.

PADRAIC, *stripped, with a bag over his head is brought in by the* CORPORAL *and* PRIVATE. *His exposed body is foul and bloody. The soldiers' manner is relaxed — they have cans of beer in their hands.*

Over there, please.

The soldiers stand PADRAIC *against the wall, his hands above his head. He sags and the* PRIVATE *beats him until he stands upright.*

Intelligence Officer Serjeant!

Voice Off Sir?

Intelligence Officer Audio-augmentation, please.

A high-pitched whining/buzzing noise commences.

Carry on, Corporal Bones, let me know when you get anything.

The INTELLIGENCE OFFICER *strolls aside, studying a 'Teach Yourself Irish' handbook, reciting simple phrases aloud.*

Corporal Your name's not sodding O'Leary, your name is fucken Teague —

Private You ran that fucken lorry over the Border on an unapproved road —

Corporal You brought ten ton of gelignite into fucken Enniskillen —

Padraic No — no — no — !

Corporal Don't you speak to *me*, you fucken cuntstruck bastard — !

Private You fucken answer the man when he asks you a fucken question! And keep your fucken feet still! Gord, how the bugger's trembling. Here, have a feel.

PADRAIC *collapses.*

Corporal On your feet, Teague, your fucken *feet* —
Private Hey, I think he's talking.
Corporal Sir, he's begun to talk.

The INTELLIGENCE OFFICER *puts up his book and comes over, crouching down beside* PADRAIC, *who is talking very fast inside the bag.*

Padraic Life-Tenancy Agreement never knew that that bastard meant *his* life always thought it meant *his* life, the Honourable's, his life till his death, his death his death not ours, when mammy went to Mass every week of *her* life so she did and only seven-fifty no class of compensation at all...

Corporal His mother and the fucken Church, it's all they ever talk of.
Intelligence Officer No good. Wait!
Padraic (*still in the same stream*) In every generation the Irish people asserted asserted their right national freedom sovereignty six times during three hundred years asserted it in arms in arms their national right in arms their national right in arms their national right to bear arms...

Intelligence Officer Ah, that's more like it. Come on, son, I'm afraid you've had rather a bad time but it's all over now. I want you to tell me quietly just what you — oh God, we've overdone it. Jesus Christ, the man's dead! Get him out of it, and keep quiet. Serjeant — will you switch off that blasted machine!

The mechanical noise stops.

Dear goodness, what a mess. Think of something, quick. Aha, yes: I have it...

The SOLDIERS *carry out* PADRAIC'*s body.*

Intelligence Officer (*sings*) [Air: *The Gray Cock*]
    'Upon a dark and murky midnight
    South of the Border but a little short way
    They bring him out and there they leave him:
    Let those who find him do what they may.'

The two SOLDIERS *re-enter from the side opposite to the one where they went out: they carry the body — or rather a dummy resembling it. The bag has gone from the head. The body is covered with tar and feathers. A large piece of paper stuck on the chest reads 'IRA VENGEANCE: INFORMERS BEWARE!' They tie the body upright to a post, the arms above the head.*

Corporal That's it then. Back to Enniskillen and not one word to no-one. Open your mouth and we're in the fucken glasshouse!

Exeunt.

Enter, after a pause, TERESA *and* SIOBHAN *in mourning.*

During the following speech they cut down the body and carry it away.

Intelligence Officer (*in tones of a TV newscaster*) A spokesman for the Department of Justice in Dublin has stated that Padraic O'Leary of Kilnasleeveen, whose body was found by local people beside a road in County Cavan, is known to have had connections with a subversive organisation and it is assumed that his death was the result of internal disputes within the organisation. The Taoiseach Mr Lynch has repeated his condemnation of all such organisations, which, he said, are not only illegal, but a deterrent to investors of foreign capital in the national economy...

Exit INTELLIGENCE OFFICER. *A drum taps a slow march.* MULHOLLAND *and a* VOLUNTEER *(in black berets and paramilitary gear) enter carrying* PADRAIC *(the real actor) laid out on a bier under the tricolour flag. They set the bier down.* TERESA *and* SIOBHAN *re-enter. They silently lay out a funeral meal on a shelf or table, over which they have draped a black cloth.*

Mulholland (*giving formal funeral oration*) We indignantly repudiate the insolent slander that Padraic O'Leary was done to death by members of the Official Republican Movement. Rather do we accuse the criminal aggression of the so-called security-forces that occupy the Six Counties. We are proud to accord a soldier's salute to this brave martyr who has gone from us.

MULHOLLAND *fires revolver shots in salute.*

SIOBHAN, *who has stood well back in silence, now suddenly comes forward and sings, with an angry emphasis.*

Siobhan (*sings*) [Air: *The Sash My Father Wore*]
'He has *not* gone from you — he was dragged
And torn away to die:
They murdered him in darkness
With a blindfold round his eye:
They butchered him like Connolly
Or Emmet or Wolfe Tone
Or a thousand thousand other ones
Who likewise are all gone!

The martyrs that you shout about
Roll over in their graves

But those alive you do not know
Bewildered work like slaves —
They cannot tell for whom they work
Or why they draw their pay:
All that they have is martyred bones
And glorious names to praise.

I will not praise my brother's name
I will not weep one tear
I will not name the nation
That betrayed and laid him here.
He came back home from Manchester
With a new word in his mouth:
They stopped that word and murdered him
Before he let it out.'

MULHOLLAND *and the* VOLUNTEER *bow to* TERESA *and go out.*
A pause. SIOBHAN *and* TERESA *stand in silence of grief.* PADRAIC,
as a dead man, sits up on the bier.

Padraic (*sings softly*) [Air: *The One-eyed Reilly*]
'They have killed me dead and laid me down
They have covered me up and buried me under
The men of power and pride confide
I can never arise and blow them asunder.
    Giddy-i-ay giddy-i-ay
    Giddy-i-ay I am dead for certain
    Giddy-i-ay tiddle-iddle-oo
    How many more like me?'

Enter BAKER-FORTESCUE *with a letter.*

Baker-Fortescue A most horrifying letter from Timothy Hagan — the
Tintawndub has been blown up — my Chalet has been blown up!
And he has the nerve to offer me what he calls a fair price for the
site!

Enter HAGAN *with a roll of banknotes which he holds out to*
BAKER-FORTESCUE.

No sir, it is not enough!

Hagan Sure it's more than ye'd get from anyone else with the political
implications that are in it. Will you not sit down quietly like a sensi-
ble man now and —

He sees TERESA. *He holds out some money to her.*

Oh, Mrs O'Leary, ma'am, some of the neighbours got together and
deputed me to give you this — 'tis the price of the fare to England.
You have a sister in Wolverhampton...? Sure ye do.

Baker-Fortescue You must double your offer, sir!

Hagan Begod I will not.

> PADRAIC *has slipped in behind them: he gives a covert blow to* HAGAN, *who thinks it is* BAKER-FORTESCUE.

> If you dare to lay hand on me I'll reduce it be forty percent!

> PADRAIC *repeats the same business to* BAKER-FORTESCUE.

Baker-Fortescue So you add to your extortion, sir, a physical assault!

> *He pushes* HAGAN.

Hagan Bedad I've flattened a better man than yourself with me left fist tied behind me — come on come on —!

> *He snatches a custard pie from the refreshment table and throws it at* BAKER-FORTESCUE.

> Not one more penny outa me, I'll take hold of your bloody paddock and squat in it meself — ho ho will ye evict *Hagan*?

> *He throws another pie.*

Baker-Fortescue No sir, oh no — you are not to get away with it!

> *He throws a pie at* HAGAN.

> Ha, you have not the advantage of having de-nazified the whole of Germany!

> *More pies.* HAGAN *tries to dodge, slips in a fallen pie, and hurts his leg. He rolls in agony.* BAKER-FORTESCUE *lands on top of him and secures the banknotes.*

Baker-Fortescue
Take yourself off, sir, and think yourself glad
I have let you get away with what you have had.
Hagan (*to audience*)
Had he chosen to behave with some common respect
God knows the height of the price he would have been able to
    collect.

> HAGAN *hobbles out.*

Baker-Fortescue Considering I got the property for nothing, I suppose I've not done too badly.

> Meanwhile I will continue and continue to look out
> Ever and about for what I can obtain:
> The main chance is now in Europe, not in Ireland —
> Not any more in Ireland — never in Ireland — no never again!

> *As he is about to leave,* PADRAIC *slips another pie under his feet, and he makes his exit in a grostesque tumble.* PADRAIC *begins to*

sing and dance, arm in arm with TERESA *and* SIOBHAN, *who join in the refrain.*

Padraic (*sings*)

'Let him go to Germany France or Spain
Or anywhere else in the whole of Europe
He'll find no rest from the likes of me
Crowding around him the whole of his journey.

Giddy-i-ay we'll crowd him round
Giddy-i-ay he can not withstand us
Giddy-i-ay tiddle-iddle-oo
We'll finish him before he's done!

When you act in a play it is easy to say
That we shall win and never be defeated
When you go from here it is not so clear
That power for the people is predestined.

Giddy-i-ay but don't forget
Giddy-i-ay you must remember
Giddy-i-ay tiddle-iddle-oo
There are more of us than them!'

Exeunt.

Methuen's Modern Plays

Jean Anouilh	*Antigone*
	Becket
	The Lark
	Ring Round the Moon
John Arden	*Serjeant Musgrave's Dance*
	The Workhouse Donkey
	Armstrong's Last Goodnight
	Pearl
John Arden and	*The Royal Pardon*
Margaretta D'Arcy	*The Hero Rises Up*
	The Island of the Mighty
	Vandaleur's Folly
Wolfgang Bauer	*Shakespeare the Sadist*
Rainer Werner	
Fassbinder	*Bremen Coffee*
Peter Handke	*My Foot My Tutor*
Frank Xaver Kroetz	*Stallerhof*
Brendan Behan	*The Quare Fellow*
	The Hostage
	Richard's Cork Leg
Edward Bond	*A-A-America!* and *Stone*
	Saved
	Narrow Road to the Deep North
	The Pope's Wedding
	Lear
	The Sea
	Bingo
	The Fool and *We Come to the River*
	Theatre Poems and Songs
	The Bundle
	The Woman
	The Worlds with *The Activists Papers*
	Restoration and *The Cat*
	Summer and *Fables*

Bertolt Brecht	*Mother Courage and Her Children*
	The Caucasian Chalk Circle
	The Good Person of Szechwan
	The Life of Galileo
	The Threepenny Opera
	Saint Joan of the Stockyards
	The Resistible Rise of Arturo Ui
	The Mother
	Mr Puntila and His Man Matti
	The Measures Taken and other Lebrstücke
	The Days of the Commune
	The Messingkauf Dialogues
	Man Equals Man and *The Elephant Calf*
	The Rise and Fall of the City of Mahagonny and *The Seven Deadly Sins*
	Baal
	A Respectable Wedding and other one-act plays
	Drums in the Night
	In the Jungle of Cities
	Fear and Misery of the Third Reich and *Señora Carrar's Rifles*
	Schweyk in the Second World War and *The Visions of Simone Machard*
Brecht ⎫ Weill ⎬ Lane ⎭	*Happy End*
Howard Brenton	*The Churchill Play*
	Weapons of Happiness
	Epsom Downs
	The Romans in Britain
	Plays for the Poor Theatre
	Magnificence
	Revenge
	Hitler Dances
	Bloody Poetry

Barrie Keeffe	*Gimme Shelter (Gem, Gotcha, Getaway)*
	Barbarians (Killing Time, Abide With Me, In the City)
	A Mad World, My Masters
Arthur Kopit	*Indians*
	Wings
John McGrath	*The Cheviot, the Stag and the Black, Black Oil*
David Mamet	*Glengarry Glen Ross*
	American Buffalo
David Mercer	*After Haggerty*
	Cousin Vladimir and *Shooting the Chandelier*
	Duck Song
	The Monster of Karlovy Vary and *Then and Now*
	No Limits To Love
Arthur Miller	*The American Clock*
	The Archbishop's Ceiling
	Two-Way Mirror
	Danger! Memory!
Percy Mtwa, Mbongeni Ngema, Barney Simon	*Woza Albert*
Peter Nichols	*Passion Play*
	Poppy
Joe Orton	*Loot*
	What the Butler Saw
	Funeral Games and *The Good and Faithful Servant*
	Entertaining Mr Sloane
	Up Against It
Louise Page	*Golden Girls*
Harold Pinter	*The Birthday Party*
	The Room and *The Dumb Waiter*
	The Caretaker
	A Slight Ache and other plays
	The Collection and *The Lover*
	The Homecoming

	Tea Party and other plays
	Landscape and *Silence*
	Old Times
	No Man's Land
	Betrayal
	The Hothouse
	Other Places (*A Kind of Alaska, Victoria Station, Family Voices*)
Luigi Pirandello	*Henry IV*
	Six Characters in Search of an Author
Stephen Poliakoff	*Hitting Town* and *City Sugar*
	Breaking the Silence
David Rudkin	*The Sons of Light*
	The Triumph of Death
Jean-Paul Sartre	*Crime Passionnel*
Wole Soyinka	*Madmen and Specialists*
	The Jero Plays
	Death and the King's Horseman
	A Play of Giants
C.P. Taylor	*And a Nightingale Sang . . .*
	Good
Peter Whelan	*The Accrington Pals*
Nigel Williams	*Line 'Em*
	Class Enemy
Theatre Workshop	*Oh What a Lovely War!*
Various authors	*Best Radio Plays of 1978* (Don Haworth: *Episode on a Thursday Evening:* Tom Mallin: *Halt! Who Goes There?;* Jennifer Phillips: *Daughters of Men;* Fay Weldon: *Polaris;* Jill Hyem: *Remember Me;* Richard Harris: *Is It Something I Said?*)
	Best Radio Plays of 1979 (Shirley Gee: *Typhoid Mary;* Carey Harrison: *I Never Killed My German;* Barrie Keeffe: *Heaven Scent;* John Kirkmorris: *Coxcombe;* John Peacock: *Attard in Retirement;* Olwen Wymark: *The Child*)

Best Radio Plays of 1981 (Peter Barnes:
The Jumping Mimuses of Byzantium;
Don Haworth: *Talk of Love and War:*
Harold Pinter: *Family Voices;* David
Pownall: *Beef:* J P Rooney: *The Dead
Image;* Paul Thain: *The Biggest
Sandcastle in the World*)

Best Radio Plays of 1982 (Rhys
Adrian:*Watching the Plays Together;*
John Arden: *The Old Man Sleeps
Alone;* Harry Barton: *Hoopoe Day;*
Donald Chapman: *Invisible Writing;*
Tom Stoppard: *The Dog It Was
That Died;* William Trevor: *Autumn
Sunshine*)

Best Radio Plays of 1983 (Wally K Daly:
Time Slip; Shirley Gee: *Never in My
Lifetime;* Gerry Jones: *The Angels They
Grow Lonely;* Steve May: *No
Exceptions;* Martyn Read: *Scouting for
Boys*)

Best Radio Plays of 1984 (Stephen
Dunstone: *Who Is Sylvia?;* Don
Haworth: *Daybreak;* Robert Ferguson:
Transfigured Night; Caryl Phillips:
The Wasted Years; Christopher Russell:
Swimmer; Rose Tremain: *Temporary
Shelter*)